Gener ...tn

'A good book about faith will make the uncommitted reader wonder about the possibility of seeing everything around them in a new way. Giles Goddard has written a very good book about faith – about his own journey, about the journey of a usually confused and fearful institution, but above all about the journey into a different, more demanding and more fulfilling vision for human beings and the world they inhabit.'

The Most Revd Dr Rowan Williams,
former Archbishop of Canterbury

'Giles Goddard has long experience of working on spirituality and diversity. This book brings together his work on climate, environment and inclusion across faith traditions. It skilfully weaves in personal stories, including his own, to the complex story of a faith community in central London. It is a wonderful resource for everyone – from spiritual seekers of all traditions to policy makers and decision makers.'

Professor Jagbir Jhutti-Johal, Professor of Sikh Studies
at Birmingham University

'This is a bravely honest, yet gracious and generous, book. It is many stories intertwined: growing up in an overshadowed family, finding a place in the leadership of the Church of England as a gay man, seeking God, campaigning for social and environmental justice, and creating a welcoming community at St Johns, which embraces people for who they are. We can all find parts of our own journey in this book, whoever and from whatever faith or philosophy we are.'

Rabbi Jonathan Wittenberg, Senior Rabbi,
Masorti Judaism UK

'This book offers a kaleidoscopic reflection on a Christian journey, of moments and movements, suffused in colour and sound. The times covered in the book reach towards the future and stretch back to the past. Throughout, we hear the winsome curlew's call, the rhythmic throb of the city, the pulse and heartbeat of the people. I was drawn in by an elegiac tale of Jacobean wrestling with self and God, at the chances and challenges of life. This autobiography is also the tale of the life of a city church wrestling with the lives of the people coursing through it and the life of the building itself. It is a tale of self-discovery, painful and joy-filled, and of vocation, ministry and mission. The reader is drawn into the warp and weft of life's tapestry, the weaving together the threads of loss, loneliness, disenchantment, dislocation, flaws, failures, self-loathing, deepening self-love, and sexual and religious awareness and awakening. Despite the fragility displayed in the text, it radiates with acceptance, resilience and hope. It is a deeply honest book, beautifully written.'

Rt Revd Dr Rosemarie Mallett, Bishop of Croydon

Generous Faith

Creating Vibrant Christian Communities

Giles Goddard

CANTERBURY
PRESS
Norwich

© Giles Goddard 2024
First published in 2024 by the Canterbury Press Norwich

Editorial office
3rd Floor, Invicta House
110 Golden Lane
London EC1Y 0TG, UK
www.canterburypress.co.uk

Canterbury Press is an imprint of Hymns Ancient & Modern Ltd
(a registered charity)

Hymns Ancient & Modern® is a registered trademark of
Hymns Ancient & Modern Ltd
13A Hellesdon Park Road, Norwich,
Norfolk NR6 5DR, UK

Scripture quotations are from New Revised Standard Version
Bible: Anglicized Edition, copyright © 1989, 1995 National
Council of the Churches of Christ in the United States of America.
Used by permission. All rights reserved worldwide.

British Library Cataloguing in Publication data

A catalogue record for this book is available
from the British Library

ISBN 978-1-78622-561-0

Typeset by Regent Typesetting
Printed and bound in Great Britain by
CPI Group (UK) Ltd

For Shanon

A race of humans has arisen which has managed to experience its world entirely as immanent. In some respects, we may judge this achievement as a victory for darkness, but it is a remarkable achievement nonetheless.

Charles Taylor, *A Secular Age*

The divine ordering principle of the whole is love.

Barbara Newman, *London Review of Books*,
14 July 2021

The soul exceeds its circumstances.

Seamus Heaney, *The Tollund Man in Springtime*

Contents

Part 4 Easter to Christ the King

Prologue

Rainbow Sunday, 2020

Here comes Josephine in her Sierra Leonian finest. Matching headwrap and kaftan in a riot of red and gold. Issy and Bena, the twins, are wearing the same. They're tall now, as tall as me, as tall as their sister Ire. She is on a basketball scholarship at a university in the USA after playing for England's youth team.

Here is Anthony from Nigeria, in his lime green shirt, trousers and cap. Mark has dug out his father's plus fours. Shanon has gone full Malay. He is in baju melayu, sky blue tunic bound by a sampin (a dark green cummerbund-cum-kilt), mother of pearl buttons, sky blue trousers. I am wearing my rainbow stole, which was given to me by Malcolm Johnson, one of the great pioneers of LGBTQ+ rights in the church, who was undermined and attacked for decades because he refused to be silenced.

'All actual life is encounter,' says Anne Lamott. 'Where there is no vision, the people perish,' says the book of Proverbs (29.18, AV).

St John's has a tradition that I have nourished. It happens on the last Sunday of the church's year – usually the third Sunday in November – Christ the King. We call it Rainbow Sunday. We celebrate the verse from St Paul's letter to the Galatians: '[In Christ] There is no longer Jew or Greek, there is no longer slave or free, there is no longer male and female' (Gal. 3.28).

We celebrate our friendships in the congregation, the relationships that help us to grow. The tradition predates the co-opting of the rainbow for LGBTQ+ people, and also for the National Health Service, but these multiple meanings make the festival more poignant.

The church is indeed a rainbow. The lining up at the altar is more colourful than usual. Hands stretch out to receive the bread and the wine: brown hands, yellow hands, white hands, black hands. Receive what you are, the body of Christ. Receive what you are, the body of Christ. The body of Christ. Amen. Amen. Amen.

We sing:

> Come, Holy Ghost, our souls inspire,
> and lighten with celestial fire;
> thou the anointing Spirit art,
> who dost thy sevenfold gifts impart.[1]

During the sermon, I ask people who or what they think the Holy Spirit is. It's a difficult question. Anything to do with the nature of God is a difficult question. Nonetheless the notion has fascinated people since the beginning of history. Bison were painted on walls in dark and inaccessible caves 40 millennia ago, probably as a means of invocation to help ensure good hunting.

'The Holy Spirit is like us. The Holy Spirit is human,' says Edna.

'The Holy Spirit is God,' says Edward.

Which doesn't take us a great deal further.

Shanon, the sociologist of religion, goes for a metaphor: 'It's the blood in our bloodstream.'

'She's love,' says Francoise, who knows that whatever question I ask in church, the answer is usually love.

There is a new hymn tune, written by Micaiah our organist. It reminds me of those great revivalist hymns that used to be sung in tents outside industrial towns in the nineteenth century: 'The old rugged cross'. It feels strange to have a new hymn tune by a Ugandan which echoes Victorian harmonies – but perhaps not surprising, for the influence of the redoubtable missionaries of empire has lasted well beyond their lifetimes. We have a strong partnership with Okusinza mu Luganda, a Ugandan church that shares our space. The arresting thing about their worship is that it seems to have all that I associate with worship in Africa squeezed out of it – especially when the whole congregation sings the Hallelujah Chorus from memory at the carol service. They are more traditionally Anglican than I am, standing up straight and singing Victorian hymns.

Many Ugandans are vocal in their resentment of what they see as unacceptable revisions to the gospel that they received. Uganda is notorious now for the homophobic laws the government has introduced. But not all think the same. The people who come to St John's are without exception warm and welcoming of me, and Shanon, and Daisy, and Eleanor, and all the other LGBTQ+ people in the congregation. Not least because many of them have experience of homophobic violence in their own land. The sister of one of our congregation had a gay son; a gang came to their house to attack him; his mother had a heart attack and died.

The complexity of our lives is real, and immediate, and hurts. There is always a time of silence after the congregation have received communion. Today, it is more profound than ever, and stretches on for more than two minutes. After the notices and singing 'Happy Birthday' and the final blessing, there is a bring-and-share-lunch. Food is brought in vats and pans and Tupperware boxes. Mark has brought apples from his orchard, and late plums. Winifred has brought ginger beer, which she made herself this morning. Rebecca was up early to make goat curry, which she has carried here on the bus, in a big tureen, still warm. Josephine has a vat of joloff rice, richly red and deeply spiced and delicious. There is sweet banana puree, Danish pastries, quiche, strawberry tarts, vol-au-vents, green salad, beef stew, more rice, chocolate cake, chocolate and banana cake. Four tables are overflowing. The queue for lunch stretches round the church and has to be marshalled by me. 'You were behaving like a headmaster,' says Shanon later.

Thirteen years have passed since I became the vicar. It has been a hard and complicated time. The UK is turning its back on organized religion; the picture in London is more complex, but even here the thing I spend my life and time doing is, to most people, not much more than a source of mild curiosity.

Nearly 30 years have passed since I became a priest. It's been a winding path, but, looking back, there is a discernible direction underlying the route I've travelled for decades. I have fought to reconcile the shadows of my life with the spotlight that shines upon me as a priest. I have wrestled with the Church of

England, at times almost to the point of giving up and leaving. I have struggled to understand what it is about the notion of God that continues to engage me.

It has been a journey from dissembling to authenticity, from presenting a false self to finding a truer self. I have, gradually, over the years, peeled away skin after skin of protective material, a carapace I had constructed in the misguided belief it would keep me safe. I have had to learn again and again, often painfully, the truth that I can do nothing on my own. The community of people in which I find myself is a community of fellow pilgrims who, given half a chance, pursue the quest for truth with conviction and delight. Through them, I have learnt how essential it is that the vulnerabilities and fragilities that I worked so hard to conceal should be allowed to be open to the air and visible.

'What *is* truth?' asks Pontius Pilate, in the account of the crucifixion story in the Gospel of John. This book tells the story of my quest to answer Pilate's question, through the increasingly strong conviction that everything is *not* relative – that there are absolutes that provide, in Paul Tillich's phrase, the ground of our being, and help us to live lives that are both fulfilling and loving.

There are two interweaving strands: my own journey from alienation and loneliness towards integration and hope, navigating the Church of England's particular canyon of rapids, and the urgent challenge to the church of how to live meaningfully in an increasingly indifferent world. The two strands weave around each other because I have been struggling to make sense of my multi-layered role – as a gay man in a religious institution that is heavily constrained by its past, and as a priest in a global city dominated by, in William Wordsworth's words, 'getting and spending'. Each strand has its own timescale, chronological or cosmic. Each strand has its own characters, although some appear more than once because everything is interlinked – and some names and details have been changed, to protect confidentiality.

One overarching lesson: none of this journey would have been possible alone. The community in and around St John's has changed too. The congregation has risen to challenge after challenge, quietly and collectively finding solutions to problems and deepening its ties of affection, with all its members finding different ways to follow their own paths. In the well-known Ubuntu phrase, 'I am because you are.' Or the Xhosa greeting, 'I see you.' So this book cannot be just about me. It has to be about St John's, Waterloo as well.

Underlying the story is the repeating cycle of Anglican worship, which is structured according to the church's liturgical year. It bridges the cosmic and the quotidian. So I begin with the First Sunday of Advent, the beginning of the Christian year.

PART I

Advent

I

The first candle

Advent is the dawn of the Christian year. A season of light,
starting four weeks before Christmas, not long after the clocks
have gone back and the nights have drawn in. That first Advent,
a dark November in 2009, I was trying to get used to the space.
To find the light in the murky gloom. We held services and sang
Advent carols: 'Christ, be our light, shine in our hearts, shine
in the darkness.' There was an Advent wreath that had four
candles, three purple, one pink, and one in the centre, white.
It was placed on a little table by the high altar, and we lit one
candle every week to symbolize the weeks before the arrival of
the Christ-child.

When I go down to the river I watch the waters running to
the sea and the cormorants perched on pleasure cruisers, their
wings stretched out to dry, looking like crucifixes. I wonder
what Wordsworth would think if he was transplanted today
to Westminster Bridge. Waterloo and the South Bank, a mile
from the Square Mile, inundated by the tidal surge of consumption. The rush of rush hour, crowds crossing Waterloo Bridge
in the twilight, I had not thought greed had undone so many,
the alienation, the loneliness.

Between the early 1980s and the turn of the century the
churchyard was part of Cardboard City, a temporary home for
people without homes: tents were head to head across the grass,
fires at night flickered on the gold mosaic on the side of the
church:

ALL MAY HAVE IF THEY DARE TRY A GLORIOUS LIFE OR GRAVE

Developers now buy and sell land at millions of pounds per acre and wrestle with residents and councillors to produce yet another tower to overtop the forest already crowding around us. Bus drivers press the secret combination to use the special bus drivers' toilets. Street drinkers piss behind the tombs.

At an early meeting of the Church Council, packed into a meeting room of the hostel next door as we had no rooms in the church, I asked them about their hopes and dreams.

'What's your vision for the future? What do you think this church should be?'

There was a silence.

'We're a friendly church,' said Holly eventually. 'You know that, darling, don't you.'

'Indeed you are,' I said. 'But what else are you? What kind of message do you want us to offer? What do you want people to find when they come to us?'

A silence.

'Not sure,' said Elaine. 'We're doing OK, aren't we?'

'Is that all we can hope for?' I asked. 'Is that why we're here?'

When the bishop granted me my licence as priest-in-charge of the parish, I thought I knew what my task was: to produce results. To renew the church and to reduce the suffering of people in need. But I had a deep fear that it would all turn out to be a waste of time and energy. There were many times when I went into church and felt that for all the work and effort and imagination and dreaming, nothing really changed. The congregation remained fragile and diminutive and their painful insecurity seemed close to the surface and unassuageable.

It felt as though I was locked in a battle between meaning and despair, between love and hate. A cosmic battle between God and the devil, and a personal battle with the demons whose especial task was to undermine me. It seemed to be a battle against shape-shifting enemies. The inertia and destructiveness of tradition. The insidious and overwhelming power of class, race and privilege. The muddied hopelessness that I saw so often in the faces of people I spoke to – drinkers ground down in the churchyard with their brittle laughter; people who appeared in church who had been struggling for most of their lives with abuse or addiction. The stolidness of the buildings I had inherited, which defiantly resisted the work of the spirit. I remembered the words of the prophet Isaiah:

> A voice says, 'Cry out!'
>   And I said, 'What shall I cry?'
> All people are grass,
>   their constancy is like the flower of the field.
> The grass withers, the flower fades,
>   when the breath of the LORD blows upon it;
>   surely the people are grass. (Isa. 40.6–7)

St John's is built on the tidal plane at the heart of London, only protected from flooding by the Thames Barrier. Sea-level rises will put this part of the city at risk; salt water could quickly inundate these streets that have been reclaimed from tidal mud. The threat of global disruption is increasing and the fragility of the city is becoming more and more apparent. What seems lasting is fleeting. We are here for a moment and then we are gone.

I am part of an institution that has a history going back nearly five hundred years, since Henry VIII promulgated the Act of Succession in 1534. A history of dark and light, times of oppression and times of transformation, an arm of the state at times and at others a critical friend. Notorious, now, as an institution that fails to welcome marginal groups and is still a long way from being fully inclusive and affirming.

I became the priest of a church that has been here for nearly two hundred years, and, climate change permitting, could be here for another two hundred. Sometimes I wondered what I could do to help it last so long – and at other times I wondered whether it even deserved to survive.

I soon began to understand that people washed up at St John's with a suitcaseful of reasons. Some came to use the loos that nestled in the vestry by the high altar. Some came because they were passing and wanted to nip in to say a prayer – often they were young and from a Catholic country where popping into church is more commonplace. Some came to see the building and to check out the architecture or the gaunt picture of the crucified Christ above the altar. Many came because they were musicians, playing in orchestras or singing in choirs.

Some came to find what they could, seeking a way to heal their pain, to deal with the damage of their early lives – or damage from their treatment by the churches they had grown up in – or because they had fallen out with God but could not silence the whisper of the Divine in their hearts.

People came to pray and sing and eat morsels of unleavened bread; they came with an ache acknowledged or unacknowledged; they came with hunger, sometimes hunger unknown; they came to seek; they came in fear, they came in hope.

They asked me questions about faith and God. I was often unsure how to answer. Was I flawed or fraud? Or both? The quietly benevolent facade I presented felt like a stage set, all columns and pediments and reliability and niceness. It was hard to know where the public merged into the private. I listened to the questions and a big part of me wanted to cry, 'Please don't trust me, it's not worth the risk. I am acting a part that the institution demands of me.'

I was already aware of one problem with being the vicar: often when I tried to be of help, the boundaries I tried to set were pushed and pushed until I had to call a halt, so my original intentions were undermined and I felt worse than useless.

The Church of England felt like an unsafe world where I was accepted only conditionally, on sufferance. The self I had constructed over many years from earliest childhood felt tenuous, a uniform, a product I had developed so I could do the work I thought I had to do. There were times when it felt as though the whole thing was about to collapse, when even my presence at St John's was under threat.

I had an atavistic fear of being found out. Impostor syndrome? Perhaps. The fear that the curtain would be drawn back and everyone would see the little old man working the machinery. The self I presented to the church and the world was as the good gay, the honest broker, the safe pair of hands. I tried to hide the toxic bifurcation between public and secret which stirred and bubbled beneath the surface. I was not always successful.

2

Walking the dog

1962–1978

On the surface, my childhood was extraordinarily blessed. I remember above all the abundant open spaces around me. Our house was large, and sat on a hill overlooking the valley of the River Rother in West Sussex, with views to the South Downs. The garden was spacious and wide, and from the fence at the boundary I watched the setting sun casting its soft glow along the shadows of the Downs. There was a grove of big pine trees beyond the swimming pool, with stacks of old fencing that I used to build camps deep in the undergrowth. My best friend Richard and I stole biscuits – bourbon creams and garibaldi, also known as squashed flies – from the tin in the kitchen, and smuggled them to our camp and munched them secretly, surrounded by the scent of pine trees.

There was a gate through the hedge beyond the kitchen that led into a patch of uncleared scrub and bramble. I disappeared there with my book and lay on the rabbit-nibbled grass under hazels and willows reading *The Lord of the Rings* or whatever novel by Neville Shute had grabbed me. Or I took the dog, Zazie, for a walk on to Hesworth Common. For years, I went every day, just me and the dog, and I rarely saw anyone, and it felt like the common was all mine, every inch. I walked through the holly wood, dark, filled with the sounds of pigeons and sometimes the cackle of a jay, and through the pine trees, the ground soft with fallen pine needles, and up the sandy slope to the Jumping Stone, where I stood at the top of the hill and listened in the early dusk to the engaging song of the yellow-hammers chattering in the silver birches. Sometimes from the distance a cuckoo called.

On the far side of the hill there was bracken, taller than me, and there were secret paths that I was sure only I knew. There was a quarry, near the road, hard to get into, but once inside I found dank standing water and the wreckage of an old car. Often I went there and felt utterly, happily alone.

No one seemed afraid, then. We went out on bikes, separately or together, me and Richard and Peter and Simon – up to Little Bognor and beyond, high hazel trees coppiced and coppiced again. Sometimes we had to crouch by the edge of the road to avoid the sand-filled lorries descending from the quarry hidden deep in the wood. Or I went, alone, into the woods beyond Bignor Hill and found my way into long rides through the chestnut plantations, where I would ride my bike – a heavy Trent Tourist restored by my father – recklessly through the trees.

This I remember first about my childhood, the enormous sense of space and freedom – the ability to escape from whatever it was in the house and spend long days out, creating a life for myself far from anyone else, far from the anger and far from the unspoken pain.

Even in the house, a Victorian villa that had grown from being a cottage to a rambling house with an extra staircase for the servants, I could hide. I was given the loft for my train set. I climbed the ladder and pulled it up after me so no one could reach me, and then squeezed out of that attic and into the next one, dry and dusty where the bodies of dead flies on the sill of the round window went untouched year after year.

I had two parents and two sisters and a dog. I was sent to the local primary school – Fittleworth, Church of England – and then won a scholarship to a prep school nearby, which I remember as a happy place, nestling in a manor house with a duck pond near the Downs. Muscovy ducks merrily had sex in front of the parents, to the Polish groundsman's dismay. We wore grey corduroy shorts and Aertex shirts, and carried out physics experiments with wires and light bulbs, and went for biology walks along the riverbank. I became a passionate birdwatcher and went out with Dr Oldham and a group of other boys to spot seabirds – sanderlings and redshanks and an abundance of curlews in Chichester Harbour. Nothing was wrong. All was good.

Except it was not. Why do I remember above all the escaping from the house, and why do I not remember family outings and the meals together and contented times with my parents and my sisters?

The stream beneath the surface was full of bitterness and unrealized hopes. Undercurrents of mistrust and resentment lay around the house like fog around tree trunks. Tension instead of joy, a limey bilious green the colour of contempt, or anger colouring the house red. My sister running into the bathroom to escape the fury of our parents; my father nailing the door shut so that she could not escape.

Behind all that lay the barely mentioned tragedy. The heartbreak that bound my parents together and drove them apart. The child whose shadow blew over us like a toxic mist.

Underlying my childhood was a slower, deeper flow: the river of history. There was a narrative that my mother and my father embraced, on which I was nurtured. It formed part of my story from my earliest years. At the drop of a hat, thick folders would be produced from the files hanging in the cupboard in the study, or from the bottom drawer of my mother's desk. The folders set out in painstaking detail the family trees of the Goddards, the De Lacy Bacons, the Barkers, the Inglises, outlining the various combinations of ancestry that had, generation after generation, led down to John Goddard = Susan de Lacy Bacon: Issue, Nicholas (deceased aged 3), Katharine, Delia, Giles.

The illustrious ancestors were highlighted and annotated. None of them especially illustrious, in truth; both my parents came from long lines of colonial clergy and the armed forces. We were formed by the Empire. A smattering of generals and bishops in the nineteenth century: Bishops of Barbados, Nova Scotia, Perth (Western Australia). The general in charge at the Siege of Lucknow, who had to be relieved of his charge before the siege was lifted. There had also been land; we were connected, but no one quite knew how, to the Premier Baronetcy, the Bacons of Norfolk, and to a long-sold country estate held by the Wiltshire Goddards.

My parents made a little go a long way. When I was ordained, my father presented me with a photomontage of portraits: Bishop Hutton of Barbados, his father Bishop Hutton of Nova Scotia, Bishop Parry of Perth, Sir William Pepperell the first Governor of New England, Major General Sir John Inglis of the Siege of Lucknow, and their wives. Louisa Hutton is particularly beautiful, with fine lips and well-kempt black ringlets. She wears a full, long summer dress and carries a parasol.

'These are the people you should seek to emulate,' he said, and in the centre of the montage is a quote: 'Let us now praise famous men.'

My mother's grandparents had been 'comfortably off'. They moved from their mansion in Sussex to a mansion in Herefordshire, for Sussex was, in 1910, becoming too suburban. The house in Herefordshire took on the status of El Dorado to my mother. 'My grandmother called all her footmen James.' 'We had to go to the Home Farm to collect the milk every morning.' 'The cook gave us secret feasts in the kitchen.' My mother's father, Lieutenant Cedric Oswald Henry De Lacy Bacon (Streaky), died of tuberculosis when my mother was six, leaving the family with a naval widow's pension. Six years later her mother married a wealthy man, Captain Boswell, and they bought a house with an orchard, called Funtington Hall. As a girl, Mum was on the edge of Court circles and appeared momentarily in the *Tatler*, one of the beautiful De Lacy Bacon sisters.

The tension in our house. My sisters, I thought, had formed a united front. The family dynamics forced me into alliance with my mother. As the replacement for a perfect son I had a role to play: to make up for the tragedy by being better than the dead child. I remember the pressure I felt to be the child my mother wanted. I was fed the story of faded grandeur and lapped it up, trying – and failing, as things turned out – to be the worthy son from a worthy family.

'We aren't the nouveau riches,' said my father, 'but the ancien pauvres.' He laughed, unconvincingly. On holidays in England we drove through the West Country, stopping at the Goddard Arms in Clyffe Pypard and staring regretfully down the drive at the unprepossessing house that had once been the family seat.

The English caste system, underpinned by the depravations of imperial extortion. Childhood photos have a background of large houses, ponies, tennis, tea parties and Morris Oxfords. Keeping up appearances. We loved the house we lived in. But we could barely afford to remain there. A sort of genteel servitude: slashing back hedges every weekend, paying the gardener and the cleaner, managing the funds that never seemed quite enough, living beyond our means, drawing down timely inheritances from bachelor uncles, always surviving, never quite thriving.

* * * * *

My early forebears had not become rich through buccaneering or the slave trade. Most of them had not become rich at all. They were, in different guises, public servants, ministers, soldiers, sailors. But alongside the veneration of the ancestors was something more insidious. The Hon. Lady Inglis, in her eyewitness account of the siege at Lucknow, gives expression to that curious Victorian combination of a high sense of calling and casual oppression. They had imbibed the nineteenth-century narrative of the white man's burden, the responsibilities of power. The conviction that the British served the colonies well, imposing a benevolent rule to transform the lot of the benighted blacks and irresponsible Indians.

On the positive side, a sense of public service. On the negative side, the failure to acknowledge the piracy and plundering legitimized under the flag of the British Empire.

Neither of my parents would have considered voting Conservative. Liberalism was their creed. My father was a founder member of the Social and Liberal Democratic Party, the potentially transformational party that emerged in the mid-1980s hoping, like so many third parties, to break the mould of British politics. He was a parish councillor and a churchwarden. My mother was clerk to the governors of the primary school.

'You've received a great deal, Giles,' said my father. 'It's time you started to put something back.'

Aged 11, or 12, I was set to work on a project at school. I was given a purple folder, illustrated with Victorian black and white engravings. The engravings showed ragged children pulling carts of coal in mines deep underground. Girls selling matches on muddy street corners. Boys being forced up chimneys to sweep them. The project was called 'Shaftesbury and the Working Children'. It told the story of the Mines Act of 1842, which outlawed the employment of children in mines, and the subsequent gradual outlawing, driven by the Earl of Shaftesbury's determination against the odds, of child labour.

The project changed the way I understood the world. Now, when I visit Clapham and pass the church in the middle of the Common, I bow to Shaftesbury and those evangelical Christians who, hearing the call to justice implicit in Christianity, fought for better conditions for the newly industrialized urban poor. That church in Clapham is now replete with conservative Christians who work in banks. It has moved a long way away from the passions that drove Anthony Ashley. But the legacy is good, and stretches down into Waterloo, 170 years later. The vertical spiral: past and future, meeting in the infinitesimal now. The past touches the present.

Through all that ancestry, I received a respect for the power of the institution: parliament, the police, the armed forces. The church. I internalized the notion of public service, of duty; of those old-fashioned words that carry historic weight. At the same time as feeling alienated and a misfit, lost in my own insecurities and my own shame, I also felt part of a bigger narrative that stretched back down the centuries – which, in the 1960s and 70s, had barely begun to question its assumptions of power and privilege. This stream of history emerged from the underworld, was instilled in me at home and at school, and formed my identity as a middle-class white Englishman. I had a strong and unquestioning sense of entitlement.

There were other streams, too, tributaries that surged underground, creating rapids, whirlpools, dangers of drowning. I have a powerful memory of the quarry in the woods above Little Bognor. We were taken there when I was about ten years old, in the school minibus – a rattling, white Comma with

long, slatted wooden seats. We were on an outing as part of an
English lesson. We had to write a composition describing the
quarry. I wandered away from the rest of the class, to the edge
of the sandstone cliff high above the excavators and diggers,
deep in the side of the hill. To a ten-year-old it was huge, and
the machines crawling around below seemed frightening and
alien. The desolation of bare cliffs of yellow sand slashed out of
the green forest was heartbreaking. I wrote a piece, now long
lost, which drew praise from Mr Appleyard as he read it out in
front of the class. I had a rare feeling of pride. An achievement
that had drawn me and engaged me and, even at ten years old,
resonated with something inside me.

It was harsher when I arrived at Lancing – described by
Evelyn Waugh as 'a minor public school of ecclesiastical temper
on the South Downs'. My sense of those years is more of feeling
like an outsider, mocked or excluded or trying to be part of the
boys' talk around me and failing. Early on I was torn apart by
the growing recognition that I was 'queer'. Too unhappy to be
able to be out and proud, in those days when pride in sexuality
was a new concept. The Tom Robinson Band's hit single 'Sing
if you're glad to be gay, sing if you're happy that [this] way',
sung raucously in the houseroom by boys for whom it was all
a bit of a joke. Danny, David, Larry and John heading off to
the five-bar gate for a fag at break, me following, trailing after
whoever it was, Danny I think, the boy with the golden eyes
who drew me sometimes up to the science block for furtive
fumblings in the store cupboards.

The loneliness of those years at school was something I barely
recognized at the time. I had, always, a sense of not knowing where I fitted. I could pass as an intellectual but I did not
study or work hard enough for that to be sustainable for long. I
wasn't musical enough to be a star in the music school, or tough
enough to be one of the hard boys who smoked and caused
trouble in class. I moved from circle to circle – the smokers,
the clever kids, the musicians – and in each circle it felt as if I
stood on the edge and looked in. It was visible to others. The
bullying had an edge of contempt. 'Drifter', they called me,
because I drifted along behind the others. I was supposed to be

top of the class. If I applied myself I could do well, but I rarely did.

My self-image was of a romantic outsider. I fell in love, over and over again, and broke my heart trailing futilely after the boys I loved. My friend Andrew fell for me and wrote me poems. He combined them into a play, 'To a slang horse' (GG), which the headmaster banned when we tried to put it on. Andrew and I read too much Hermann Hesse. We listened to Wagner late at night and walked in the dark across the South Downs looking down on the lights of Lancing and Shoreham. The burning need for love: I feel it now, looking back. Not slaked by cold embraces in dark corners of the school. Something more was painfully absent, and I had no one whom I dared explain it to, even if I had been able to find the words.

I found myself living a double life. The emotional entanglements, the crushes, the rejections, the bullying: all that had to stay secret. Only Andrew heard it, and his life and mine were unhelpfully tangled. Beyond that, no one. I became adept at hiding my feelings, staying alone, living in secrecy. I learnt to separate the public from the private, the open from the secretive, the presented from the actual, the conscious from the subconscious. Here were planted the seeds of the bifurcation that caused in later years such harm.

Perhaps that was one of the hardest things for people growing up queer in the days when the stigma hurt like an unhealed scab over an open wound. So many of us had no one to speak to, no one to tell us that unrequited love happened all the time to teenagers, no one to stand up for us when the bullying started, no one to hug us when the hurt became too great.

The drowned boy was often in the back of my mind. Unmentioned but unforgotten. The lovely 3-year-old in his sailor suit smiling brightly at the camera. Compared with him, I was sure I was a disappointment. Hopeless.

3

The second candle

The lighting of the Advent candle was a little ceremony. Holly loved Advent, and so did all the children – especially Bena and Issy. They both stuck their hands up quickly when I called for someone to light the candle. Issy was the younger of the twins, with a gentle sensibility. She was a foal, all limbs and flexibility. They, and Lola and Ella and Oisin, were gathered with me around the Advent candles. Bena got to light the taper and held it to the second candle, purple. It guttered into life and we said the opening prayer, the great Collect for Advent Sunday.

> Almighty God,
> give us grace to cast away the works of darkness
> and to put on the armour of light,
> now in the time of this mortal life,
> in which your Son Jesus Christ came to us in great humility.[2]

On the Second Sunday of Advent we remember especially John the Baptist. He appeared in the wilderness, according to Matthew's Gospel, wearing a coat of camel hair and living on locusts and honey. I have eaten locusts; they taste a little like prawns. The combination with honey seems both tasty and nutritious. And camel hair is soft; so perhaps John was not quite the ascetic that history makes him out to be. Perhaps too he was not the sexy young man painted with such relish by Caravaggio. But he was a man with a mission, and he challenged the powerful. 'Repent,' said he, 'for the reign of God is at hand.' Advent time, the wilderness season, John the Baptist out there in the desert, only a few scrubby trees for shade, trying to find his place, speaking to the crowds who flock to hear him. He incurs the wrath of the powerful for he speaks truth to them. He tells them to share their wealth with the poor, to end the Roman soldiers' and tax collectors' extortion of the people of Israel. He is a prophet, a mould-breaker, an inspiration for me.

In this purple season we sing hymns in the minor key. 'O come, O come, Emmanuel! Redeem thy captive Israel!' Advent is a time to repent. In the run-up to Christmas, that period of extreme consumption, we are asked to live simply, to remember the mistakes we've made, to acknowledge our descent into greed and selfishness. In Waterloo we are surrounded by the baubles and brashness of Christmas even though we are in the heart of Advent. We live a double life, acknowledging the darkness but living in the light.

Beneath the church lurked a place of darkness. Down the stairs that led to the crypt, a door stood locked. Soon after I arrived I unlocked it and went in. There was a stench: foetid air unchanged in months; the miserable smell of damp. A chill crept into my bones. Feeling around beside the door I found the light switch. Fluorescent tubes flickered into life, revealing a long, high, narrow brick space, gracefully arched but disgracefully filled with the detritrus of decades. A table tennis table squashed against the wall. A slab of concrete with half a mosaic speckling the surface, reminiscent of a Blake drawing of paradise or hell. A coat rack of mouldy clothes, red velvet damp and decaying. Old beer barrels. I kicked one – empty.

The door was locked to my own subterranean darkness too. I had some idea of what lay behind it. I knew that it was a shadowy place touched by tragedy. It was not somewhere I wanted to explore. I had no torch, and the corridors and little spaces were full of skeletons and decaying remains of broken relationships. I knew I would have to unlock the door soon, for I could not expect the building and the congregation to be honest if I did not permit my own truth to see the light. Particularly in the season of purple, the colour of the shades at dusk.

The space I occupy has been occupied by many before and will be occupied by many who will come after. The air I breathe has been breathed before. The water I drink has been drunk before. And the place where I stand, behind the altar, has been stood in by a thousand people before.

London's oldest human artifact can be seen at low tide not far from Vauxhall Bridge. A few blackened stumps, perhaps the relics of a quay or the footings of a long-lost bridge dating back 6,000 years. Much later a Roman road crossed the river here, taking troops from the warm Mediterranean south to the freezing Hibernian north, or bringing them hurriedly home again.

The river ran shallower and wider then, not dammed by high embankments or squeezed under bridges. At high tide, the entire marshy basin between the forested hills was flooded. Pewter-grey water reflected winter clouds. There was silence except for the wind's sighs, the grunts of foraging animals, the harsh creak of black-backed gulls, and sometimes the urgent whistling of a flock of curlews.

Layers of history lie beneath much of the city. A Roman amphitheatre under the Guildhall, the dark hollows of the hypocaust still visible, the shouts of spectators almost audible, the arena where beasts fought and humans sacrificed easily traced. Plague pits around Smithfield. Foundations of the Rose theatre buried deep inside an office block on the river's Southwark bank. Not far from here, hard by Caffè Nero in the Oxo Tower, is another causeway, exposed when the water recedes, used for centuries – millennia – for the launching of boats to cross the fast-flowing river.

But the marsh remained marsh while the city grew around it. Between Southwark and Lambeth the reign of mud continued long into the seventeenth century. The first attempt at reclamation, a dyke along the riverbank, did little to contain the tides. Beneath the steps of St John's, beneath the neoclassical portico lending its pomposity to the bus station and the IMAX cinema, there are few relics. No broken bits of blue and white pottery, no empty earthenware flagons, no discarded oyster shells, no bones, human or otherwise.

The relationship between water and church is symbiotic. Below the building is the water that gives it life and strength. The water of life flows – seeps through the clay, maintains the humidity, keeps the tower standing. The water that once flowed along the muddy creeks and every twelve and a half hours drowned the mudflats, nourishing the abundance of cockles and whelks and mudworms that made their home there, is the same flow that nourishes the ancient soil and keeps the building upright.

The world keeps turning, regardless of human presence. Until not very long ago the sea invaded the creeks twice a day, regular as the moon, drowning the mud and sedge and reeds. As the brine withdrew, a high-stepping curlew curiously tipped over stones and investigated under plants with its finely curved bill until it was put up by a marauding wolf. It and its flockmates took to the air shrieking. Their whistling echoed across the flat mud towards the glowering hulks of Westminster Abbey and the Cathedral of St Paul, brooding above the huts and houses across the river.

The spirit of the curlew is still there, beneath me. If I am silent and the church is quiet, and if I listen very carefully, I can almost hear the bubbling call, the chatter of the flocks as they move en masse along the edge of the water, probing and piercing their crescent bills to find juicy worms and delicate sandcrabs.

The Eurasian curlew was once one of the most abundant birds in estuaries such as the Thames. *Numenius arquatus* – the genus and the species was named in the eighteenth century by a contemporary of Linnaeus, part of the passion for categorization that captured European intellectuals at that time. The name of the genus *Numenius* is poetically derived from the shape of the bill: *neo* means new, and *mene* means moon. So the bird that obsesses me is named for the moon, which defines the tide of the church's year, the arrival and departure of Ramadan, the date of Passover, the festival of Nowruz. Truly, everything connects.

The plangency of the bird has long been recognized. The anonymous poet of the 'Seafarer' writes, sometime in the tenth century, of the hardship of life on the sea.

There I heard nothing except the thrumming sea,
   the ice-cold waves.

Sometimes the swan's song I kept to myself as diversion,
the cry of the gannet and the curlew's voice for the
  laughter of men –
the seagull's singing for the drinking of mead.
Storms beat the stony cliffs there,
where the tern calls him with icy feathers.
Very often the eagle screeches with wet feathers.
No sheltering kinsfolk could comfort this impoverished spirit.

The poem was collected in the *Exeter Book*, which has been in
the possession of Exeter Cathedral since 1072. The seafarer is
a pilgrim, called to forsake the wine-comforts of the city and to
seek the way that promises him rewards in this life and in the
life to come.

My heart is restless within me,
my mind is dwelling on the sea-flood,
over the whale's domain.
My mind fares widely over the face of the earth,
but returns unsatisfied. The lone-flier screams, urging my
  heart
to the whale-way over the stretch of seas.
For the joys of the Lord are more inspiring
than this dead fleeting life on earth.

The UK is one of the most important habitats in the world for
the curlew. Hundreds of thousands of breeding pairs used to
throng the mudflats and fields of Britain and Ireland, sending
their calls across moorland and marsh. The heartbreak is this:
the curlew is now on the red list for endangered species. In Wales,
the population has declined by over 80 per cent since 2006,
and across England numbers are down to barely 100,000. The
decline is due almost entirely to the loss of breeding grounds;
curlews make their nests on the ground, in scrapes, where they
incubate their eggs for four weeks. Intensive agriculture, drain-
ing marshland, and the predations of foxes and crows and
dogs have meant that few eggs survive to hatch, and of the few
chicks who hatch, even fewer reach adulthood. The call, once

frequent, is now rare. I hear it, sometimes, when I go to Suffolk, to the reserve carefully created by the RSPB at Hollesley. The sound of it is no longer joyful but sad.

On the Third Sunday of Advent the third candle was lit by Oisin. This one was pink, in honour of the Virgin Mary. Advent is supposed to be a time of remembrance, a reminder of our need for love. But it has lost its preparatory meaning; symbolized by Advent calendars that contain behind each door a liqueur chocolate. A penitential pina colada. Consumption trumps asceticism. The ancient fast is blanketed beneath the modern feast.

Here in Waterloo, here in the Global North, we have been seduced by the notion that we can walk away without consequence, we can reboot our lives and wipe the hard drive clean of the sins that, from time to time, we most grievously have committed. We have become drunk on over-confidence. Man is the measure of all things. Leonardo's image of the *Vitruvian Man*, naked, arms out wide, encloses in his outstretched limbs the dimensions of the world.

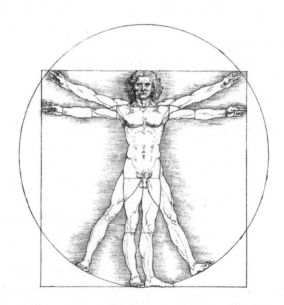

I began to wonder, as I tried to make sense of the place where I had washed up, whether the battle I was locked in was really between love and hate, between God and the devil, or whether it was something more insidious – a battle between love and indifference. The Church of England, a relic from a more authoritarian time, now reduced to little more than a club for misfits, perceived as a place of unwelcome, especially for LGBTQ+ people.

That opened up an even more challenging question: how can I – we – speak of meaning in a universe that is seemingly unconcerned, where the world keeps rolling onwards and onwards through space regardless of our momentary struggles and hopes?

In Waterloo, the call of the curlew is silenced. I want to hear it again, whistling softly across the winding marshland paths.

PART 2

Christmas to Epiphany

4

Eternal moment

2009

The choir was rehearsing hard for the carol service. We had a
room in the crypt which we reclaimed from David the revolu-
tionary mosaicist a couple of years after I arrived. All rent is
theft, he told me when I asked for his rent arrears. He vacated
his studio to create a new degree course in mosaic-making in
Camden. We named it the Mendelssohn Room, because Felix
Mendelssohn is rumoured to have played the organ in the church.
I passed the door and heard the choir sing, 'The Angel Gabriel
from heaven came ... O highly favoured lady.' I remembered
the joke from junior school: 'O highly *flavoured* lady', as if
she were a milkshake. I had shared the joke with Shanon who
shared it with the choir, and now I heard them singing it and
giggling.

'Lilian needs communion for Christmas,' Maureen said. She
had just turned 80 and had bright red hair. She had been Akela
for the Cub Scouts for 25 years until she retired on her eightieth
birthday. She also ran the 4C's Bingo on Wednesday evenings
at St Andrew's, and produced Stephen, Keith and a clutch of
grandchildren, all pale and white like plants grown in a cupboard. She married Tony the Scoutmaster back in the 1960s
when he was a mod and she was a mod's girl. They lived on
the Octavia Hill Estate for the whole of their married life –
tiny model houses for the deserving poor, created by Octavia
Hill in the early twentieth century and sold, shockingly, to the
highest bidder by the Church Commissioners at the start of the
twenty-first century. Tony was very deaf towards the end of his
life but refused to give up work. He often shouted at the Young

25

Vic when they came in for rehearsals. Much oil was poured on troubled waters by Lorraine, our business manager.

'You stick to your vows, Giles,' said Maureen. 'You've married the man, haven't you, and you stick to what you said.' After Tony died she started coming more often to church. 'You're the first person who's ever asked me to get involved,' she said. My heart ached.

I'm fond of the family. There's a sister, Pat, who was shocked beyond imagining when I swore during a game of Trivial Pursuit. 'You can't say that! You're the vicar!'

I've never been allowed to forget it. Her proudest memory, an anecdote that resurfaces often, is of dancing on a table in a bar in Turkey, powered by Bacardi and Coke.

'Fine, I'll take communion round,' I said. Lilian was the third sister. She lived in one of the Octavia Hill flats. The carers were leaving when I arrived on Christmas Eve bearing the sacrament – the wafers, already consecrated and so the body of Christ, which we keep in the tabernacle in church for exactly this kind of need – in a little silver pyx. The carers curtseyed to me as they left. The TV stayed on while I tried to talk to Lilian's daughter Mary. The flat was tiny and overfull with trinkets from seafront shops and old newspapers and well-stuffed cushions. It was too hot and the TV was too loud.

The bedroom was stuffy, windows closed; Lilian was diminutive in bed, wearing a pink nightdress, her bedside table covered in pill bottles and tissues and a plastic drinking cup with a spout.

'Mum! Mum! Giles has come to bring you communion!' Mary tried to wake her. She rose out of sleep like the slide of a whale's back but disappeared back down into the deep. Mary tried again. Lilian had had Parkinson's for ten years and dementia for five. She couldn't be woken. The flat felt sad, tight, trying to make something out of nothing; it's a hard thing dealing with the slow death of a parent.

I left, and came back later. She was a little more awake when I returned, enough to half-register my presence. Richard was there this time, her partner of 30 years. He's a devout Anglo-Catholic, head server at another church, with an eye for detail like a trainspotter. He had cared for Lilian faithfully ever since she began to disappear. I realized that my coming was more for Richard and Maureen than it was for Lilian, but I was glad to be there. I did a super-quick bedside communion in case she should go back to sleep, stumbling over the Lord's Prayer. She barely responded, but when I passed the wafer to Richard and he passed it to her, she opened her mouth to receive it. I had brought a tiny chalice and some wine; Richard held it to her lips – perhaps she recognized the smell – she swallowed greedily and finished it. That'll help her dreams, I thought, and reflected on the deep recognition that still existed even when the mind seemed to have gone on a long journey. The richness of repetition, the resonance of celebration, even if all the outward surfaces of response are reduced to a slithery smoothness. I wondered if the act of receiving communion somehow eased her unconscious mind. She took the chalice to her lips with familiar ease, but the years of training in taking only a sip were forgotten. Good for her, I thought. I was glad I went, that Christmas Eve.

2014

Midnight Mass. Darkness. The first verse of that carol about David's city, sung by the choir in the dark. We light the candles of the people at the end of each row and a warm light spreads through the building. The singing is half-hearted at Midnight Mass; we have unfamiliar people, tired and sometimes a little merry. At last the fifth candle in the Advent ring is lit, the white one at the centre, and we begin the service in the comforting glow of candlelight.

Hand-held candles become slippery and hard to hold after a while, so early on, with the reading of the tale of the birth of the Messiah, they are extinguished. Electric light keeps darkness at bay, and I begin the great prayer of consecration over the bread and wine. I elevate it at the end of the prayer, holding it high for all to see. This is the one time of the year when we sing the final verse of 'O come, all ye faithful':

Yea, Lord, we greet thee,
Born this happy morning,
Jesu, to thee be glory given![3]

It is not until everyone has received the body and blood of
Christ that the lights are extinguished, the candles are relit and
we sing, quietly, in fatigue and relief, 'Silent night, holy night.
Sleep in heavenly peace.'

A few years after I arrived, there was a mini-row. Belinda had
produced beautiful flower arrangements high on the windowsills,
of holly and ivy, with candles embedded to create a pathway
of light towards the altar. She brought her family to Midnight
Mass, partly to see the decorations. But the servers had not
lit them. I realized, halfway through, and scampered towards
them with a lit taper. They were too high up and I needed
a ladder and the service must continue. Belinda was gravely
disappointed, and afterwards the complaints were loud, and
heartfelt, and I felt bad for her and bad for the church. This was
not the spirit of Christmas I was seeking, and in the vicarage
there were recriminations. The small things matter. The flickering of candles in the darkness.

I stand on a Sunday morning and I look out across the congregation. Each person holds desire, identity, loss, alienation.
Their eyes meet mine in a moment of fear or a moment of trust.
Some of their secrets I know, others have kept things locked
away in their hearts.

I have seen them holding out their hands, one by one, as they
stand at the communion rails: gnarled hands, smooth hands,
twisted hands, scarred and broken hands, hands of different
hues, arthritic hands. The hands of blind people and old people,
teenagers and trans people. I have placed a morsel of bread in
each of them, and I have looked into their eyes as I said, 'The
body of Christ', and they have looked back at me and said,
'Amen'. And I have passed on to the next person, thankful for
that moment of shared intimacy.

The richness of the moment is nourished by the depth of
the soil in which it's planted. The body of Christ seems to me
to be much more than a wafer over which certain words have

been spoken. It is the gathering around the altar of the people who come, bringing their fragile selves to share in this ephemeral but cosmic act. Communion reflects community, and both are grounded in the cumulative act of congregations across centuries.

Often I have felt the arc of history bending towards this moment. I have reflected that this might be the thirty-thousandth time that the words of institution have been said in the precise spot where I am standing:

In the same night that he was betrayed,
[he] took bread and gave you thanks;
he broke it and gave it to his disciples, saying:
Take, eat; this is my body which is given for you;
do this in remembrance of me.[4]

It might be the twenty-billionth time those words have been said, somewhere in the world, in some language. They are taken from Paul's letter to the Corinthians (1 Cor. 11.23), and Paul knew well the Hebrew scriptures that stretch back a thousand years before the time of Christ. I am still awestruck. I am using phrases that were first used 2,000 years ago and come from a tradition dating from a thousand years before that. All encapsulated in one uncatchable moment when I place the bread in Kate's hands and she, being blind, receives its touch and brings it to her mouth and says, 'Amen'.

All of time and all of eternity collapses into a moment shorter than a quantum burst. The vertical meets the horizontal. Past embraces future in the present. I learnt from Carlo Rovelli's book *The Order of Time* that time is neither linear nor vertical nor even cyclical. Time stretches out for each person towards the future and the past. Each person experiences their own time. It's a little like an hourglass, stretching towards infinity at top and bottom, with each of us representing the waist point. The hourglasses intersect when we meet or when we engage.

I have a duty to the past and a duty to the future. This broken place with its kaleidoscope of disorganization, the jigsaw puzzle awaiting re-creation. I am on the cusp between yesterday and tomorrow, trying to live today as if it mattered, perching on a momentary timeline. I have been given responsibility for the place and its people: to hand it on in as good heart as when I found it – at least as good, and better, if possible. I hold the present, a filigree globe, glittering in the palm of my hand. A moment. My time, your time, the world's time, God's time.

The archaeology of earth, buried century by century, layer upon layer. The quiet presence of the past below us, the layer-cake of soundscapes. This church, I am fond of saying, has been here for two centuries and God willing it'll be here for two more; but the gurgle of evening song from the robin on the musk rose has been calling across the brackish marshland since the river first emerged from the hills, unsmeared by human feet. Beneath me time stretches deep into the centre of the earth until it rests at the infinitesimal point of stillness.

5

Born again

Religion played little part in my life as a child. Sunday school, sometimes: I have a clear memory of colouring a picture of St Paul on the road to Damascus, using a crimson crayon to fill the bright light that struck Paul with blindness. Lancing had High Anglo-Catholic traditions in a Gothic revival chapel 180 feet high, standing proudly on the Downs by the A23 between Brighton and Worthing. I sang in the chapel choir and enjoyed the rousing Victorian tunes. But my religious awareness was not awakened, and I had little sense of touching the numinous.

Until, suddenly and without warning, I was invaded by Christianity.

'Giles,' said Adam, 'my family and I go, every summer, for a week's house party. It's held at a school near Tunbridge Wells. It's a Christian house party. Would you like to come?'

Adam was one of those friends whom I tried to keep secret from the tough boys smoking at the five-bar gate. His father was one of the masters. The family was notoriously religious, running the Christian Union and hosting Bible studies in their home. We were friends because we both sang tenor in the chapel choir. Adam was thoughtful and hard working, and we did our homework together. His parents welcomed me into their house, and I went gladly to tea, but I kept that friendship quiet when I was supplementing my allowance by smuggling carrier bags full of cigarettes from Shoreham back to school and distributing them to my customers.

I had never been to a house party before. It sounded fun. A week in a school with access to all the facilities – swimming pool and tennis courts and lawns under cedar trees. I saw the programme – regular worship and Bible studies. I thought I could live with that.

I remember the week as unremittingly sunny. Families of well-spoken people with their children at smart schools arrived in Rovers and Jaguars. I went on the train, on my own, across Sussex – a daring journey – and carried my suitcase from the station. The young people were placed in dormitories in a house down the road from the main building. We gathered, on the first day, for worship. We were arranged in an informal circle on orange plastic chairs in the main hall. At the front, a small band. Guitars and drums, and a singer with a microphone. The words of the choruses were displayed on an overhead projector, acetate slides being replaced one after another by the man responsible for the technology. There were eyes closing around me, faces being lifted towards the heavens. This was a new experience. I was uncomfortable. It was a very far cry from the sombre hymns and understated psalms of Lancing, even when Neil the organist was letting rip and the high windows of the chapel were rattling. Here were middle-aged men in shorts and open-neck shirts beginning, as the choruses went on, to raise their hands and to smile in ecstasy, with their wives in flowery dresses and their children lifting their hands too. Adam caught my eye.

'Welcome,' he whispered. 'We're so glad you're here.'

The story drew me in. We all became firm friends in a matter of days. Jeanette and I went for long walks along sunny railway tracks between high hedges, getting out of the way of trains as they shot past towards Eastbourne or Hastings. The young people opened their hearts to each other. I became friends with Lucian, from Winchester, slender and beautiful. He took me aside one evening, in the boys' dormitory.

'Giles,' he said, 'I have something to tell you.' He took my hand. 'I've been queer. And I don't like it.'

I felt that I too could confess.

'Lucian, you're not alone. So have I. And I don't like it, either.'

'But I know that God loves us, whatever we do, and forgives us. If we pray hard enough.'

This was the hope I was looking for. An end to the loneliness and alienation of those teenage years. I learned that many of the people there were from a church in London, I had not heard of, called Holy Trinity, Brompton. A community of good and decent people, mostly rich and smart, but with abundant social consciences. We prayed, often, for those in other countries who were starving or suffering, and the poor and homeless in our own nation. They seemed to be open to accepting me as I was – and they opened up the possibility of change.

I leapt at this promise of new life. Four days in, on the Thursday evening, we gathered for worship at the end of the day, in the main hall. The choruses kicked off. The music surged and swelled. The spirit began to move. Arms went up. Muttering began around me, incomprehensible words under the breath, respectable men speaking in tongues. I began to feel that the time had come. I wanted to join this crowd of people and I had been told the password. All I had to do was to invite the Lord Jesus into my heart, and I would be saved. There we are. It's as simple as that.

I told Adam I was nipping out to the loo. I went outside, through the kitchen, and into the open air by the garages. I leant against the wall of the garage, my head resting on my upraised arm. I looked at the tarmac in the half-light, and spoke the words I knew I had to speak. 'Lord Jesus, I give my life to you. Take me and make me yours.'

There were no blinding lights or angels, no sudden arrivals of tongues and celestial choirs. But I did have a feeling of relief and a burning delight in my heart. I went back in, doing my best to look transfigured, and stood next to Jeanette. She looked at me, and I smiled back.

'I've done it. I've asked Jesus into my life,' I whispered to her. A smile lit her face.

'Giles! Thanks be to God! We must tell everyone!' She embraced me quickly and went to the front, where her father was singing, leading worship. She interrupted and whispered to him. He looked over at me, and mouthed 'Praise be!'

As soon as the chorus ended, he said to the assembled worshippers, 'I have something to share with you. We have a new Christian! Giles has given his life to Jesus, tonight!'

The abundance of praise and the unfeigned welcome were enough for me. I was, for that moment, at the heart of this new community. I thought I had come home. The sense of belonging was real and powerful. Almost subversive, as, the following term back at school, we began to criticize the chapel hierarchy and scoured the scriptures to discover how to live well. We had long and complex discussions about predestination – the belief that God had fore-ordained all those who were to be saved and that we were part of the saved remnant – a doctrine that seemed at best unfair and at worst positively wicked. No matter, we should take such things on faith. The most important thing was giving thanks to God for his great love for us. And holding to the principles of righteous living.

For a year or so, it felt good. It was not so much the power of the worship: I was never slain in the spirit as so many are, when they become part of charismatic worship. I could never pray in tongues, and felt inadequate because of my failure. But I was glad of the enlargement of my world and tried to live the life I thought I was called to live.

2011

Two years after I started at St John's, I spent Christmas Day with Delia, my sister, and Tony, her husband, and all the nephews and nieces and all the Clark cousins in Mill Hill. The rule of the Clarks was that everyone got everyone a present but the maximum spend was around £5. There was a riot of unwrapping and an avalanche of shining paper revealing packets of pepper and salt from Borneo, and herbs and mugs and cheese boards and jam and honey and socks and more socks and mittens for toddlers and Lord knows what else, and there was conviviality and delight.

Nobody mentioned the incarnation. Tony's family is originally Catholic but mainly atheist now. Religion is weird, to be mentioned if at all with perplexity and in hushed tones. The children were at non-church schools and had little acquaintance with the Christmas story. Nobody mentioned love, but for all of us here gathered that was the metatext, writ loud down the long table with the abundance of special diets – gluten free, vegan, dairy free. For me, fully omnivorous. It was Christmas, after all.

Nobody mentioned our mother, who was in Suffolk, brought from her home in Saxmundham to Katie, my other sister, and her family for Christmas Day. Perhaps we had mentioned her enough before. Perhaps there was no more to be said. She wasn't well enough to travel. Her mind was going, slowly. It's not Alzheimer's, I told people, it's vascular dementia. She was confused and forgetful but her feet were still on the ground and she was fully aware of what was happening around her; fully aware and highly critical.

Christmas is the time of good intentions. We have left purple behind and dressed the altar in gold, we fill the church with flowers after the barrenness of Advent, we gather around the manger to celebrate a birth, we remember the poor and the homeless and give donations to charity and sing Christmas carols under the clock on Waterloo Station, and there is peace and goodwill to all. But the thorns in our sides are still there and the pain and anguish are still there.

So, privately, I remembered my mother, with whom my relationship is full of hurt and disappointment, and who would I knew be remembering her first son.

It was at Christmas that it happened. When my brother was three years and four months old. Our parents had left him in the care of our grandmother and had gone to London to see a play. My grandmother had a big garden, more of a park. The step-brothers of my mother, who were around 12 years old, were playing in the park, and the au pair was inside the house doing the things that au pairs do, and each thought that Nicholas was being looked after by the other, and he was playing by himself, and he fell in the pond and drowned.

His death was always present. There were photos of him in the house: in one in particular, I have it here, he is in a sailor suit, standing on a five-bar gate, leaning back and smiling into the camera, his hair tousled and his eyes clearly blue even in the black and white photograph. His smile is open and trusting, his shoes tiny and laced, and if you look closely you can see in the distance an elephant.

I can see his little body, face down in the pond.

My mother rarely talked about him. Once she spoke, shortly after my father's death, when she was more open than she has ever been to me, before or since. She spoke of the phone call to her sister's house in London, of the drive through the night back down to Little Bognor in Sussex – what must that have been like; my parents, who were at the time on the point of divorce, rushing down the A roads through the darkness in their rattling Morris Minor, arriving at the house and going into the kitchen?

'There he was, laid out on the table. They had done his hair all wrong. It didn't look like him. I've never forgotten it. I thought for a moment it wasn't him.'

One year, when she was more than usually negative, I had taxed her. We had tried to give her a good Christmas but the tension and the sourness barely lifted. Angry, I asked her, 'How much longer will you grieve for him?'

'Giles, you never forget. It hurts, always.'

I said, feeling hurt that I and my sisters *still* weren't enough, 'He died 50 years ago. Surely you can move on?'

But you don't. You never forget. Especially at Christmas.

6

The daily round

2014

A midwinter morning. Sun slants across the churchyard and long shadows of plane trees fall against the warm yellow brick of the church. I have wrapped up because the church is cold at this hour. Luis is doing what he does every day with deep commitment, raking the paths in the churchyard, capturing every stray leaf and plunging it into the darkness of the compost heap. I greet him as I fumble with my keys and unlock the side door, making my way into the Lady Chapel, where, as ever, Eileen has been busy since half past seven.

The church is silent at that time in the morning. No orchestras or project managers or theatre companies, or homeless people praying for their dads. The chapel is, like everywhere else, a little shabby, and the green glass from the windows gives me a sense of drowning. It is my turn to lead Morning Prayer. I take out my book, a red book, *Common Worship: Daily Prayer*. It has six ribbons, of different colours – red, green, blue, yellow, purple, black. At the front are the words of the service, including the canticles repeated each day – the Magnificat, the Nunc Dimittis, the Benedictus. At the back are the psalms. We also have a Bible and a commentary.

Shanon has come too, and Georgie, my fellow priest, blows in from Roupell Street. Dwayne slips in, silent Dwayne from Peckham, wearing the same stained ochre rain jacket he always wears, smelling of the roll-up he smoked before coming in. We greet each other quietly. Dwayne has severe mental health challenges. I ask him how he is. 'So so,' he replies, as he always does. I look in the little purple book which lays out, day by day, the set readings and psalms. Bryony and Douglas arrive as I am about to start. We take our books and use our ribbons to mark the pages we'll need and, once all are ready, off we go.

O Lord, open our lips.
And our mouth shall proclaim your praise.

We say the psalms set for the day. Some we say frequently, others are reserved for special occasions, especially for Lent and Holy Week. The daily repetition is a great wonder. Verses often leap out at me as if I've never seen them before, when I've probably said them a hundred times. Today, Psalm 97 resonates with me, as it is one of my favourites:

The mountains melted like wax at the presence of the Lord,
at the presence of the Lord of the whole earth.
The heavens declared his righteousness,
and all the peoples have seen his glory. (Ps. 97.5–6)

There are psalms of praise:

Sing to the Lord a new song;
sing to the Lord, all the earth. (Ps. 96.1)

And psalms of misery:

I am counted as one gone down to the Pit
I am like one that has no strength,
Lost among the dead,
like the slain who lie in the grave. (Ps. 88.4–5)

Or, appositely enough in this age of mad autocracy, there are complaints against the people in power:

Why do you glory in evil, you tyrant,
while the goodness of God endures continually?
You plot destruction, you deceiver;
your tongue is like a sharpened razor.
You love evil rather than good,
falsehood rather than the word of truth. (Ps. 52.1–3)

They have a freshness as if they were written yesterday. We take it in turns to lead. We leave a pause at the end of the line, for one, two, three seconds. The repetition becomes rhythmic, like a chant. We read a section from the Bible, whatever is set for the day. When we toil through the grim prophecies of Jeremiah our spirits sink. When we have accounts of the stranger miracles or sections of beauty from the Song of Solomon our hearts sing. Or we grimace at some of the more gruesome images:

> Now [Judas] acquired a field with the reward of his wickedness; and falling headlong, he burst open in the middle and all his bowels gushed out. (Acts 1.18)

We read a commentary – a few paragraphs by a notable church person. We pray for the church, the world, holding whichever crisis is at the front of our hearts at the time – a coup in Myanmar, Covid deaths, Ukraine, craziness in the USA, the outworking of Brexit, poverty, homelessness, natural disaster, climate change, so much to pray for, and we pray for the sick, remembering Peter who has cancer, Rosa who is nearly 100 and, amazingly, still alive, frailer and frailer but still living in her own home, and we remember the dead – my uncle Nico, and Tony's sister Emily who died suddenly of a heart attack. We follow the prayers with silence.

The quiet stretches on – for one minute, two, three. It passes very quickly. I hear the rumbling of a stomach next to me. I open my eyes and see the others praying. My mind wanders towards the tasks I am facing during the day, or it returns to my mantra, repeated silently under my breath, from Psalm 103: 'Bless the Lord, oh my soul, oh bless the Lord.' Sometimes for a few moments I am transported to another place. More often not. But the silence is the heart of the prayer. The prayer is the heart of the day. Daily prayer is the heart of the church.

> The trivial round, the common task
> will furnish all we need to ask,
> room to deny ourselves, a road
> to bring us daily nearer God.[5]

The candles are lit at the beginning, and extinguished at the end, and we chat and bid each other a good day. I leave the chapel, closing the door behind me.

It is a routine, like cleaning my teeth. The discipline opens up the doors between worlds. Monks and nuns, clergy and laity have been doing something similar since before St Benedict wrote his Rule in the fifth century, in Umbria – they picked up the custom from the followers of St Anthony, who made his way out of Alexandria and into the desert in the second century. He discovered the importance of a routine of prayer in his life of solitude among the rocks and the scrub and the jackals and the scorpions. Whenever I say Morning Prayer, I am living a tradition that has continued for nearly three millennia. But now, like so much else in the church, it is a marginal pursuit, a flickering candle in this secular world.

There are two Greek words at the heart of the Christian story: *agape* and *metanoia*, usually translated as *love* and *repentance*. *Agape* is the kind of love, I was told when a teenager, that was godly because it was not besmirched by sexual desire. *Eros* – the passionate desire of love – was not to be trusted for it could lead us astray. Such rubbish, I now realize; a distinction that was used to justify centuries of oppression, and set up a tragic imprisonment of love, which is so much more passionate than the safe sense implied by *agape*.

And *metanoia* means much more than repentance. *Meta* means beyond and *noia* means mind. So it speaks of the movement to a new mind, a beyond mind, a different place, a radical transformation. The word we translate as repentance is not really about saying, 'I'm sorry, I'll try not to do that again.' It's about saying, 'I am a new person, and the many things of which I am ashamed, the many insecurities I have, the many challenges that I face, which I am dealing with … all of these things can be left behind if I am willing to embrace the idea of love, radically and universally.'

This is the depth charge at the heart of Christianity. Not so much the arc of history; more, the radical irruption of resurrection where there was death, of light where there was darkness. The pinprick of a candle's light or the first evening star in the dusk changing everything. *Eros* and *agape* on fire. A match flaring in a cave.

Hope is different to optimism. 'This, too, shall pass.' Optimism implies a belief that things will gradually change. Hope implies a belief that, although everything seems like shit, good things will come. Optimism relies on the march of history, hope is radically discontinuous. The eruptive potential of shared humanity. Something to celebrate.

Here at St John's we push at the boundaries of orthodoxy by combining Candlemas, which falls on 2 February, with Christingle, the child-focused service that emerged from Germany in the seventeenth century involving an orange, four cocktail sticks, some sweets and a candle on the top. I like to combine them. It works at this time of the year. Before Christmas everyone is drowning in carols and light and angels and Christmas trees, but in February the lightness is welcome. At the end of the service we process around the church holding up our oranges with their lit candles, and sing a joyful hymn.

Candlemas follows hard on the heels of Christmas and Epiphany, but it is not about progress. It is not about the inexorable outworking of the dialectic. We do not proceed smoothly from one festival to the next, like the transition from spring to summer. Advent does not calmly swing into Christmas. Advent bumps up to Christmas. Suddenly purple becomes gold, and then, in the darkest time, we hold up the light of the Christchild. Candlemass is the last Sunday of gold, before we move towards the darkness of Lent. Candlemass is a moment of hope.

7

Falling away

Nicholas was always present, albeit rarely mentioned. Our private Christmas tragedy. My parents quickly had another child after his death: my second sister, Delia. And then a miscarriage. And then me. My godmother-to-be, Muriel, opened champagne on the night I was born.

'Your parents were desperate for another boy,' she told me, years later.

My father brought home flowers one day in August, when I was about ten years old.

'Why have you brought those?' asked my mother, crossly.

'Have you forgotten? Nicholas would have been 18 today.'

'Take them away, I don't want them.'

My older sister was just over a year old when he died. A therapist might be able to uncover whether the tension between her and my mother was because she had survived and he hadn't or whether there was a dysfunction in my mother's embrace of her daughters because of her own childhood, or whether it was a combination of the two, but my mother has never allowed a therapist near her.

As the youngest and the only boy, I imbibed the responsibility of being loyal to her through all the rows and all the squabbles. At birth I was given a task: to be the replacement, the awaited one, the fulfilment of my parents' broken hopes. I tried to be that person. Perhaps I am still trying. When there was tension in the house, between my mother and my sisters, I sided with my mother. I thought that was my job: to be the good boy, never quite as good as the boy who had died, but a reflection of that lost child, re-offered by the universe.

Soon after I had, I thought, given my life to Jesus, cracks began to emerge, and it began to feel as though this home I thought I had found had no roof – or walls, or a floor – in fact, it might even be a deceit. Sexuality, of course, was a presenting issue. I finally summoned the courage to speak to the group leaders. I was, thankfully, not part of the nexus of Christian boys' camps and abuse in the 1970s that has recently become public, and was never subjected to the practices now known as conversion therapy, which were in their infancy then. But the position was clear, I was told: abstinence and prayer. I called a halt to sex. I urgently prayed to overcome my crush on the beautiful Samuel in the year below me at school. I prayed for healing.

The prayer did not work. My supposedly disordered desires continued, amid increasing levels of guilt. Was I not praying enough? Was I not good enough? Was I to be condemned to a loveless life by an Act of God?

There were wider questions, too. Questions of theology. The problem of evil, the deaths of innocent children, the salvation – or otherwise – of non-Christians. We sat in fuggy studies and discussed these things. We were told by our leaders that we had to allow such questions to be a matter of faith, not rationality. The answers were in the scriptures, and the scriptures were the ultimate authority, and we should seek no further.

The cracks in the structure grew. I had a good brain, my father often said, and it was important that I used it. But here, in this house of faith, it seemed my brain was not welcome. And neither was my sexuality.

After 18 months or so, I understood that I had a choice. Between God and love. I had thought that the two were coterminous: but it seemed that this was not so. I was leading a life of irreconcilable opposites. One of them would have to go.

In the end it was simple. The one that went was God. I woke up one day and decided that I would do religion no more. And, to satisfy myself of its invalidity, I would study Theology and Religious Studies at Cambridge (if I passed the entrance exam) and would prove the rationality of atheism.

I gave up God, and was accepted by Clare College, and

planned to spend three years there disproving God's existence. When my father suggested that it might be good to use my year off to learn German, I leapt at the chance. So, in a frozen January in 1981, I found myself in Göttingen, close to the border with East Germany, living with the austere Lutheran parents of my school friend Bernhard. He was another misfit. He had been sent to Lancing because his parents were afraid he might be tempted by the radical activism of the Marxist terrorist groups of the 1970s, the Baader-Meinhof Gang and the like. They hoped a British public school would sort him out.

The house of Bernhard's parents was in a village above the city, and I took the bus each day into the Goethe Institut to learn German. The snow fell heavy on the roads. Those years at the end of the 1970s and before the arrival of AIDS and the global triumph of neo-liberalism felt, in retrospect, quite free. I discovered alternative Deutschland. Black and grimy dance clubs spinning punk in cellars in the back streets of Göttingen. Activists wearing Palestinian keffiyahs and driving VW camper vans. Demonstrations in the streets, which I joined excitedly. Passionate conversations in bars about the better world we wanted to create.

Even more exciting was the first dipping of the toe into a world of adult sexuality. Bernhard, by good fortune, had a brother who was gay, and he had childhood friends who lived locally, and they knew the way to the only gay nightclub – ze Beeg Apfel, they called it. Another life emerged, which I kept secret from my hosts and from everyone at home. I was taken in hand by a man called Horst, a couple of years older than me, a musician. The furled flower began to open. I discovered, to my enormous surprise, that people found me attractive. Before long I moved from Göttingen to Munich, a bigger city in every way. I found lodgings with Philip and Klaus, and a job at McDonald's in Leopoldstraße near the centre, and suddenly the flower erupted into a golden, enchanted bloom. I had a pair of bright yellow trousers, and a greatcoat with fur lapels which I had found in a junkshop. The streets of Munich were so clean that it was unnecessary to wear shoes. My working hours were 4 p.m. to 12 midnight, and after that we all went clubbing, or to the sauna, or to bars, and I returned home at 4 or 5 a.m., either alone or with some new friend, and slept until the afternoon when I arose, barefoot again, and walked across the city to work.

A ziggurat of experience packed into three months. New kinds of friendship. Jürgen lived in a Turkish guestworkers' hostel, on the third floor. He came from Regensburg and was a devotee of Erich Fromm. He gave me a book to read which I have still: *The Art of Loving*. He sat outside McDonalds on a sunny afternoon in June and spoke of the ways in which we damage love by fighting for our own corner instead of placing the needs of the other at the heart of our desire. But I was not ready to hear that. I was enjoying the new-found freedom to sin with impunity. I bleached my hair and inserted an earring, single, sparkling, blue. I interrailed with my friend Caroline down through Yugoslavia to Greece and back via Venice to Germany. I returned to England, boy become man, or so I thought. I found autumn leaves on the trees in the garden, and I found my mother doing her best to welcome me back.

The Petworth Festival was in full swing. An arts and chamber music festival organized by a local composer who lived in Brinkwells, the tiny thatched cottage in the hills above Fittleworth where Elgar had composed his Cello Concerto. Bob had friends from London, and with them I was able to carry on the new behaviours I had discovered in Germany. Until, after an evening of flirting in a singsong around the piano in a pub in Petworth, my mother asked me, as I sat on the window seat in the drawing room and flashed my earring at her:

'I don't know whether you're gay or not ...'

When I nodded, her face collapsed.

'Really? You really are? I don't believe you.'

'I am.'

I was sent to talk to a psychologist, and I was told that my godmother Muriel, whom I adored, would be horrified, and I was not under any circumstances to tell my father.

'If you are gay, Giles,' she said – or she may have said queer – 'it will be the worst thing that has ever happened to me – including the death of Nicholas.'

PART 3

Lent and Passiontide

8

The discipline of Lent

2012

Almighty and everlasting God, you hate nothing
   that you have made
and forgive the sins of all those who are penitent:
create and make in us new and contrite hearts
that we, worthily lamenting our sins and acknowledging
   our wretchedness,
may receive from you, the God of all mercy, perfect remission
   and forgiveness ...[6]

The most solemn time of the year begins. Lent, the period of
fasting and repentance. In Lent we wear purple. According to
the Gospel of John, Jesus was mocked by being robed in purple
and having a crown of thorns forced upon his head. Purple is a
rich colour, and was expensive in the days when the only source
of the dye was a certain breed of sea snail that lived in the Mediterranean near the city of Tyre, in Phoenicia. It is the colour of
kings and also of penitence. Perhaps that is not a coincidence.

Lent is an ancient festival, derived from the Festival of Booths
and Yom Kippur. It begins with a service on Ash Wednesday.
The crosses from last year's Palm Sunday have been burned to
create ash. The congregation gathers in the dark and empty
church, in a circle of light pooled around the altar. Solemnly,
small in the silence of the great building, we repeat the great
Litany:

From all evil and mischief;
from pride, vanity, and hypocrisy;
from envy, hatred, and malice;

and from all evil intent,
good Lord, deliver us.

From sloth, worldliness and love of money;
from hardness of heart
and contempt for your word and your laws,
good Lord, deliver us.[7]

One by one, the people line up in front of the altar, and from one to the next I go, dipping my finger in the ash, making the sign of the cross on their forehead, saying:

Remember that you are dust, and to dust you shall return.
Turn away from sin and be faithful to Christ.

Sometimes I lose concentration and invert the sentence: turn away from Christ and be faithful to sin. I get a surprised look from the person I'm ashing and have to correct myself.

I have given each person a stone as they come in, and invited them to leave the stone in a basket as they come up to be ashed, symbolizing the leaving of their shortcomings and failures behind. I hear the clink of stone on stone as they are placed in the basket, one by one. It's a powerful ritual as the weight of the sins of the year is laid down.

What you don't say rules you. Which is why it matters that we acknowledge the reality of sin. Not as the tool of oppression exploited by the church for centuries – the mechanisms of repentance becoming its preeminent source of power, the sale of indulgences, extreme penitential rites, flagellation, abasement. Not the tired and dangerous narrative that condemns homosexuality as objectively disordered, excludes women because of their complicity in the wickedness of sex, equates blackness with sinfulness. No. There is a different, more hopeful story.

What you don't say rules you. If we fail to call out the things we do that destroy ourselves and others they have disproportionate power. So, during Lent, I try to name my own grief and lament my own failings, as well as the grief and the failings of those around me. By giving something a name I open my heart to it. It becomes real. As something real it can be attacked and, potentially, vanquished. *Metanoia*.

* * * * *

I felt, when I arrived, as if I was in conflict with the building. This broken place with its kaleidoscope of disorganization, the jigsaw puzzle awaiting re-creation. It was like an unrisen soufflé. I wanted it to rise, to sing, to inspire. But I wondered if it would let me.

I called architects. I asked them to show me what they could do with the space. They came from around London, bearing plans and brochures and speaking lucidly of how the building could be. In the end we chose Eric Parry, recently accoladed for his work at St Martin-in-the-Fields, a craftsman running an atelier of architects and designers, a Rembrandt for our times.

Eric constructed a vision. He proposed a remodelling of the hasty post-war rebuilding, to lift and lighten the place, to create a new setting for the mural painted for the Festival of Britain by Hans Feibusch, the Jewish refugee, to construct a new framing for our worship on a Sunday, so that it would become a place of music and light, a place the Church of England could be proud of here in this fast-changing world of Waterloo, a place of pilgrimage and hope.

But there were objectors who didn't like it. They came in their phalanxes. They arrived and formed up like the Roman army, shields up and spears out, and they sucked the energy out of the atmosphere as they grimaced and growled and said, 'No!' The principal objector patronised us for our lack of understanding of 1950s' neo-classicism. The irony of the Twentieth Century Society breathing the spirit of reactionary conservatism was not lost on us.

Every diocese has a Chancellor, whose job it is to approve applications for Faculty. The conservation societies have the right of representation. Documents were lodged, in the Inns of Court at the Temple across the river. The Chancellor issued his Directions. He decreed that there should be a Consistory Court so that he could hear the arguments for both sides. We were pitted against our objectors and there was no turning back.

1980

The decision in my late teens to leave God behind was for my own well-being. I had been offered something that I thought was beautiful – access to the power of God, to a community of friends, to a whole that was much greater than the sum of its parts. The realization that the promises I had received were written in water propelled me into an atheist hinterland.

I discovered what seemed a better way to live. I tried to turn my back on the mystical. I thought I was like one of those German heroes battling through the pathless forest. But, to my surprise, I felt dislocated. I was neither in nor out. It felt empty. Disenchanted. There was no forest. I found, instead, desert. The desert became my home.

Disenchantment. A powerful and sad word. The end of a relationship is often described in terms of disenchantment – the loss of mystery, the shattering of dreams. 'This rough magic I here abjure,' says Prospero in *The Tempest* as he breaks his staff and he and Miranda leave the island and return to the hurly-burly of Naples. There is a comfort, though, about disenchantment. The conviction that reality has no room for such things as mystery and magic. The universe is of itself enough. No need to go beyond it. What you see is what you get.

Enchantment can be malevolent. Prospero's island was an unsafe place. Caliban, Ariel, the whole crowd were all exposed to mortal danger. They were flotsam before the manipulations of the magician. The realm of Mordor ensnares Frodo and Sam and nearly kills them. The elves of Galadriel appear beautiful but there is darkness beneath the glimmering light. Even white witches have the power to control or to destroy.

Discovering a new pride in myself as a child of the Enlightenment, a rational liberal believing in freedom – in its 1970s' sense of being free to be me rather than its 2020s' sense of being free to oppress others – I doubled down on the conviction that the arc of history did indeed tend towards justice. Surely the world would be healthier if there was none of this nonsense about religion and magic. Surely we should file the world in a box marked 'science' and rely only on explanations for which there is verifiable proof.

I think my dislocation was an attempt to maintain control. There is a connection between disenchantment and power. We dare not offer space to anything that might threaten us, especially the spiritual. Disenchantment is republican, a republic of the human. The emperor is dethroned. I am answerable to no one.

But in truth I could never quite let go. I paddled in that godless sea, afraid of drowning. I meandered from the years at school drifting after the trendy boys, to the years in London trying to be part of the *jeunesse dorée*. Resisting the idea that I might be seriously spiritual. Always the fear of not being loveable. Always the fear of not being loved. Always the loneliness. Wandering, wandering, wandering, a pinball. Unwilling to admit the possibility that there may be anyone out there who is listening to me, anything there that might receive the arrow I shoot across the abyss. The drowned child smiling at me, unreachable, across the void.

9

A disenchanted world

London in the 1980s. The long years of Thatcherism. Miners' strikes and the privatization of BT, mass shareholding, council house sales. Defeat after defeat for the Labour Party. The triumph of Friedmanite economics. The widening gap between rich and poor. New Romantics, men in make-up. Boy George, Divine. High energy. Night clubs in ornate pub ballrooms far out on the Romford Road. Donna Summer, the Communards, the Pet Shop Boys. The eruption of AIDS. The Terrence Higgins Trust, buddying people with AIDS. Condoms in bowls on bartops, policing the saunas, I will do THIS, I will not do THAT. Put on the condom and feel safe. Take the bus back to Dalston from Heaven, alone again. Lonely. Pick up an Italian boy in a cafe on Dalston High Road, his bedroom infused with the smell of halal chicken from the butcher next door. Life upon life, a cascade of unacknowledged unhappiness.

After university I became a graduate trainee for the John Lewis Partnership. It was good of them to take a punt on me. I was promoted, before long, to be Assistant Buyer in Bathroom Fittings and Glass and Plastic Kitchenware. Finding the work unfulfilling, I left John Lewis for a job in social housing, and then became Director of Development for an Asian housing association. The work was busy, but it left plenty of time for the life of a gay man in London in the late 1980s.

Lent is a time when our private struggles can be shared. Demons possess me as they possess others. I remember especially the short-term anaesthetics I sought.

The mass of men lead lives of quiet desperation. What is called resignation is confirmed desperation. From the desperate city

you go into the desperate country, and have to console yourself with the bravery of minks and muskrats. A stereotyped
but unconscious despair is concealed even under what are
called the games and amusements of mankind.[8]

Through my twenties and thirties, the search for love seemed
never ending. My first loves had been at school, the admired and
desired boys who tempted me to the five-bar gate and to nico-
tine, boys with whom I shared brief moments of ecstasy in the
abandoned car in the garages behind the squash courts. Then
came a disrupted love at Cambridge, a first relationship that
quickly soured, which hurt more badly than I was prepared to
admit. It planted a seed of belladonna which took root and grew.
I decided that I did not want to be hurt again. I played a game
of self-preservation. I found people, I formed brief relationships
with them, I said goodbye to them when I could see that affection
was growing. My identity was defined, I thought, by the amount
and type of sex I was having. This was what made me who I was,
gave me membership of my community. So whoever they were –
Konrad, Max, David, Edmund, Hassan – they were bit parts in a
narrative of identity. Useful for a moment and then gone.

I became practised at separating feelings from actions. Layer
below layer, like a science experiment where liquids separate,
red beneath amber beneath blue. I watched myself playing
games with the people I toyed with. It felt as if the self I was
constructing was separated from me by soundproofed glass. I
gave a good impression of being charming, and developed what
seemed to be close friendships, but there was a line of intimacy
I could not cross. The skills of bifurcation and shape-shifting I
had learnt in adolescence served me well. I thought I was keeping myself safe. I convinced myself I could still pass as a good
boy on the surface.

Always the shadow of a toddler falling across me like the
cartoon shadow of a giant child. Always aware of him leering
smilingly behind me in his sailor suit, the childish whisper, 'You'll
never catch up. You'll never catch up.' Always the self-preservation, the self-deception. 'Here! creep/Wretch, under a comfort
serves in a whirlwind.'[9] Unforgiven. The one who survived.

There were crushes and there were occasional longer relationships in the attempt to obtain the partnership I wanted so
much. But I did not understand how much I was sabotaging my
emotions. Unknowingly, I was turning myself into an empty
husk.

There was one relationship that lasted. With Eamonn, who
taught me loyalty: the youngest of 13, from Ireland, a waiter in
Café Rouge when I met him, thoughtful and creative and border-
line alcoholic, chaotic and caring. A crooked smile and an impish
laugh. Smaller than me, the last of the litter, with his best friend
Jerome – they decided that they were the lost princesses of the
Romanovs, Tatiana and Ivana. Sometimes I collected him from
work in the Mini I drove at the time, or from whichever council
flat he had ended up in, and we were followed home by the police
who checked my car for drugs. My friends were relieved, on one
level, and dismayed on another. I learnt from that relationship
about the need for constancy, but in the end the love we'd tried
to nurture did not flourish, and we parted.

Bernhard, my radical ex-extremist German friend, had fallen
among friars. Franciscans in their long brown habits were a
part of his life and he lived in a flat that they occupied in Dean
Street, Soho, above St Anne's Church.

'Giles,' he said, one day, hearing the tales of my latest exploits,
'I think you should come back to church. It will do you good.'

'Shan't,' I said, and thought little more about his suggestion.
But he planted a seed between the cracks, and, unknown to me,
it began to put down roots.

2017

The alarm goes off at 5 a.m. and Shanon crawls out of bed. He
goes downstairs to make his breakfast. Ramadan started yesterday. Shanon is not the most traditionally observant Muslim in
the world, but some things are special and essential to him, and
keeping Ramadan is one of them. Nothing to eat or drink from
sunup till sundown. The beginning of the month of fasting is set
by the lunar calendar, which is 11 days shorter than the solar

year; so the month moves backwards through the year. When I first knew Shanon, it began in September; it has slipped back through August and July and June, and now starts in the middle of May. So the period of abstinence is, today, officially from 05.04 to 20.50 – slightly shorter than when the month traverses the summer solstice, but a challenge nonetheless.

I try to keep the fast; but I claim special exemption as a Christian, and begin with breakfast at 7.30. I have no food or drink all day, and we break our fast together – iftar – at sunset, with a fresh date and a cocktail. I am glad that Ramadan follows shortly after Lent at the moment; Lent becomes a preparation for the greater rigours to follow. It is surprisingly easy not to eat or drink, once I've accepted that a quick glass of water or a sandwich is not an option. Even in the heat, if one remembers to move slowly, the thirst is not unbearable. By the end of the day I feel hunger and thirst. Oh yes, I think, of course I'm thirsty. I'm fasting. I count the hours, and then the minutes, and then the seconds, until the moment when I can have a sip of water and enjoy the burst of sweetness as I bite into a date. At that moment, the wait is worth it.

Sometimes I wonder if I am indulging in spiritual machismo. It reminds me of the parable of the tax-collector and the Pharisee; the Pharisee up at the front of the synagogue, praying smugly and thanking God that he is not like that snivelling tax-collector at the back; the tax-collector humbly asking God for mercy. I tell myself that I am trying to live simply that others may simply live, but I hear a voice saying, 'To fast not once but twice in the year; that sounds like pride.'

Perhaps it is. But the discipline has many benefits. I do not lose much weight, for I eat as much over two meals as I normally would over three. But fasting takes me into a different space.

Before the crucial conference on climate change in Paris in 2015, COP21, there was a pilgrimage to Paris. A motley group of Christians, and one Buddhist, set out from St Martin-in-the-Fields in Trafalgar Square on a drizzly Friday morning, to walk all the way to Paris, arriving there as COP21 was beginning. I was unable to walk the whole way, because I had a parish to run. But the five days I walked with the other pilgrims, 70 miles from London to Newhaven, was a powerful experience. We tramped through the streets of Kennington, across Clapham Common, down the A24 through Streatham and branched off into the suburbs of Croydon. Sleeping on the floors of church halls, we eventually left London, crossed the North Downs and carried on through Surrey. There is a public footpath that runs through the middle of Gatwick Airport, beneath the terminal, to the alarm of the security guards guiding 40 pilgrims with rucksacks through the rain and the dusk – but we passed safely through, and in the rain reached Sussex.

On the second day we woke to the news of the terrorist atrocity in Paris in which 130 people were killed. The pilgrimage became something very different as we walked on, not sure if we would even be allowed to enter Paris. Walking in excruciating consciousness of the failed and destructive relationships between faiths and between people, made worse by the risk of climate change. Walking to change the world.

I remember one moment very clearly. We were trudging in heavy rain through mud thick as toffee in a wood somewhere between Croydon and Crawley. We came out of the wood and started crossing a field. On an embankment above us, screened by leafless trees, ran a railway line. A train scurried by, and I caught a glimpse of a woman looking out of the window at us stumbling through the scrubby damp. It felt as though I was in a completely different world to her. Who are those people on that train, I thought, and where are they going in such a hurry, and why? In a matter of days I had shifted in my head from London to another dimension, and I had a glimpse of what it must be like to live in a monastery or to be a hermit.

Ramadan is redolent of that – more so than Lent, because it is more demanding. Hunger and thirst almost a secret, a shared experience, a chosen discipline, a refocusing of priorities, reminding us that there is a different life beyond this one, taking us into a more holy place. I am glad of it, and glad to be participating in this global discipline.

Bismillah al-Rahman ar-Rahim. In the name of Allah, the Beneficent, the Merciful.

10

The dazzling darkness

2017

On the Fifth Sunday of Lent, Passion Sunday, there is a change of gear. We penetrate more deeply into the darkness of our long journey towards Good Friday. The Gospel set for the day reads:

> 'Now my soul is troubled … Now is the judgement of this world; now the ruler of this world will be driven out. And I, when I am lifted up from the earth, will draw all people to myself.' He said this to indicate the kind of death he was to die. (John 12.27, 31–33)

The people of St John's have travelled alongside one another through the previous four weeks. Some of them have told me what they are doing, their penances, their efforts to lead a godly, righteous and sober life. Jimmy is trying to give up alcohol. It's not easy for him; I know he has a drink, sometimes much more than one drink, on his own after work, but he doesn't mention that he is also fasting, eating only one bowl of cereal every day. As for me, I announced on Ash Wednesday that I was going to try to be vegan – a hostage, if ever there was one, to fortune, as my veganism is at best sporadic. But I am pleased, because I have managed – Shanon and I have managed – to be meat free from Monday to Saturday, and as we like our food we think that we are doing quite well.

It can easily feel ridiculous. Sometimes I try to put myself in the shoes of someone who has no background in the routine of church life. The weirdness of it all. Black South London teenagers in white robes wearing black trainers (when they remember), leading the procession, carrying candles, one of them bearing the cross. Lisa or Georgie or Paul or me in our whiteness bringing up the rear while the organ swells and the congregation cranks into action. The repetition of canticles and psalms, the reading again of readings we have heard hundreds of times before, the long slow ritual dance of the Eucharist, the queuing of the people to receive a scrap of unleavened bread and a sip of sweet fortified wine. These rituals, re-formations of practice traceable back millennia, words repeated down the years, in English or in Aramaic – Hosanna! Alleluia. *Eloi, Eloi, lama sabacthani.* My God, My God, why have you forsaken me? All this, for what?

Passion Sunday is the right Sunday to ask; for over the next two weeks we will be telling a story of religiously sanctioned murder. The high priests, we are told, gave the order to arrest Jesus, and then, after his arrest, sent him to the Romans because it was not within their rights to pronounce a sentence of death. Whatever the reality of the events behind the story, the execution of a preacher and teacher on trumped-up charges by the religious establishment in connivance with the imperial power is not a happy tale, and there is a perfect irony that the Christian church, historically a collection of institutions with more power in aggregate than any others ever, should have at its heart this story of an extra-judicial killing.

But that's exactly the point. It *is* a story of murder, fear, betrayal, human wickedness, jealousy, power and control. As Roxie Hart says in *Chicago*, 'All those things we hold near and dear to our hearts.' It *is* like an opera. It takes us into the depths. But unlike an opera it takes all of us, body and soul, collectively, a community, into the depths. It is not a diversion for which we pay £120 and in which, after three hours, or six if it's Wagner, the music is done and the heroine has died.

Why do we do it? Because the story is more than a story. It's life.

1988

A few more night bus rides back from the bus stop outside the National Gallery and blurry awakenings the following morning took their toll. Bernhard's suggestion bore fruit, and one Sunday morning I found myself alighting from the number 38 in Shaftesbury Avenue, going through an unprepossessing Victorian door and up a flight of wooden stairs, following a sign that said, 'To the Church'. Hoping to creep in at the back where no one could see me.

'Good morning,' said the vicar. 'I'm Fred. What's your name? Welcome. Come in.'

I regretted coming at once.

'Umm. My name's Giles. I'm afraid of – sorry, a friend of Bernhard's. I ... umm ...' I was on the verge of flight.

'Come in,' he said, gesturing towards the door.

I entered an oak-panelled room with about 15 wooden chairs. A solid wooden altar faced me, with two lit candles. Stained-glass casement windows, gold and yellow, stood half open allowing traffic noise to permeate the room. On the chairs sat a little collection of people, waiting for the service to start. Some elderly women with wispy hair. A couple of young men in button-down shirts. A round man with a shiny pate wearing thick-rimmed glasses who came up to me.

'Welcome. I'm the churchwarden, Brian. Come in. Have a hymn book. Have a seat.'

There was no way I could escape. Bernhard was not there yet. But I saw a familiar face, someone I had met before in the flat upstairs.

'Come and sit here,' said Tim.

Fred wandered in, now wearing a white robe and green stole. He invited us to stand, and suggested that we might sing hymn number 43, 'Praise to the Lord, the Almighty, the King of creation'. I knew it well from school. He led the singing in a powerful voice. We quavered in, the elderly women and the young men – and a couple of young women who had arrived after me – and me. It felt comfortable, and before long I became less self-conscious. The worship began to take shape, and the familiar words began to resonate.

> **We have sinned against you and against our neighbours,**
> **in thought and word and deed,**
> **through negligence, through weakness,**
> **through our own deliberate fault ...**
> Almighty God ...
> have mercy upon you,
> pardon and deliver you from all your sins.[10]

It felt like a cardigan, comforting and homely. I stayed for the whole service, and then for coffee, and everyone spoke to me – Vivian and Pam and Rebecca and Anne and Tim and Brian. No one questioned me and I felt quietly welcomed – and that was that.

Tim invited me to Suffolk for weekends, to his tiny coast-guard cottage on the shingle shore dwarfed by the East Anglian sky. We ate leeks and tomatoes from Mr Maskell's vegetable garden along the strand, and we crunched on the shingle under the night sky, shivering in the north-easterly wind, and he spoke to me about love. Not in the particular but in the general sense, as a thing, a force that is real and that had the potential to bring all the pieces of me together. We read poetry together, moments encapsulated by Emily Dickinson in her wonderful ellipses:

> To make a prairie is takes a clover and one bee, –
> One clover, and a bee,
> And revery.
> The revery alone will do
> If bees are few.[11]

And William Blake:

> We are put upon this earth a little space
> That we may learn to bear the beams of love.[12]

But when I began tentatively to step back towards the church, I retained a force field around myself to resist invasion by the spiritual. It's just a story, I told myself. Whatever we mean by God, I said to myself, it's a concept, a construct, like gender or sexuality.

Tentative steps brought me crabwise into the sun, but I kept a parasol above my head. I saw the clerical establishment at work and I resisted it; I wanted never to be dependent on the institution. I roved, avoiding intimacy (the Boy Disease, as my friend Anya called it). As faith began to weave its spell again, I remained resistant. Afraid of over-committing. Of being asked for more than I could give. I tried to stay safe.

2017

Those prophets. Do we really *have* to read them, I ask, as the reading cycle for the year lands, in Lent, on Jeremiah yet again. They're so depressing!

The great theologian Walter Brueggemann in *The Prophetic Imagination*, replies emphatically, yes. He goes further, and says that the prophets in the Hebrew scriptures are essential reading for they cast important light on human experience. Their passion is enflamed by the depravity of human behaviour, particularly the behaviour of the rich and powerful. The mistreatment of the widow and the orphan, rent seeking, sharecropping, idol worship, the pursuit of power and status; this is all wickedness and must be named. Named in grief, and lamented. Jeremiah, the prophet who dared to grieve.

Eugene O'Neill said, 'Man is born broken. He lives by mending. The grace of God is glue.'[13]

The debilitation of sin is that, if unacknowledged, it leaves people in deep darkness. I struggle to overcome my resistance to naming my own sin. It is not easy to name, for it requires humility and honesty. But I am a warrior without weapons unless I can know my enemy. The devil, our adversary, prowling around like a roaring lion, seeking whom he may devour (1 Pet. 5.8).

I enter the poison cloud, the circles of hell. I listen to the scritch and scratch of the earth beneath the pavement, trying to hear the call of the curlew, digging around in my subconscious to uproot the weeds that clutch. Structurally, the Empire, exploitation, class and race privilege. Personally, the nights of prowling through clubs and saunas, the emotional emptiness, the indulgence. God, I have no need of you.

To be a pilgrim. Weeping with is weeping alongside. We walk together across the marsh, surrounded by ditches, by beasts that bite and traps that catch. The wilderness is full of noises. There are shadows beneath the trees. On the marsh it is easy to lose our way.

The hero must learn that the demons will only be slain when they are allowed to speak. He hears voices in his head which tempt him, which encourage him to slither off the side of the road and into the abyss. If he is to stay on the road he must silence the voices.

We undoubtedly fall. The question is, have we the courage to stand up again?

11

Moment of choice

1990

I was in the vestry at St Anne's, counting the collection after the service one Sunday. We were in the new building by then, constructed on the site of the old church. Fred was putting away his vestments when he murmured to me:

'Giles – have you ever thought of being ordained?'

'What,' said I, 'becoming a priest? No way!'

'You might find it quite fulfilling.'

'I'm full of admiration for what priests do,' I said, so as not to give offence. 'But I'm quite sure it's not for me. I have a good job and a nice flat. Why would I want to change all that?'

'It just might be something to think about, that's all,' said Fred, and we passed on to other things.

That seed planted refused to die. In his quiet subtlety Fred kept up the pressure.

'Have you had any more thoughts about ordination?' he asked, some weeks later.

'Yes, I have. I refuse to join a homophobic institution.' It was the time when General Synod, in a toxic debate, reaffirmed that the only permissible place for sexual activity was within heterosexual marriage. The House of Bishops subsequently produced a report that grudgingly acknowledged the existence of 'homophiles' but announced that homophile clergy 'should expect to be celibate'. To willingly enter jail? I don't think so.

But I kept finding myself repeating Fred's question, even though I tried to push it away. I began to wonder what it might involve, how it might feel to be a priest. I began to imagine that the circle might be squared, that a way through the sexuality midden might be found. I felt nagged, but there seemed to be nothing I could do to make the nagging disappear.

There was a service of evensong at St Anne's. The chapel was small, wood panelled, with a simple crucifix made by a German sculptor hanging above the altar. The service was simple, too; Fred leading, us responding.

I sat in the chapel, singing the hymns, listening to the readings, praying. But my mind was not on the service. Round and round went the question in my head.

'If I go forward, and the answer is no,' I reasoned, 'then that will be fine and it'll free me from this endless circularity.'

'But what if the answer is yes?' I asked myself.

'Then the decision has been made.'

'But what about the gay stuff? Are you really willing to impose celibacy on yourself?'

'No, of course not. But nobody really believes that gay clergy are going to give up sex. I would just have to be open, from the start, so that no one can accuse me of misleading them.'

'But then they'll definitely say no.'

'Well, if they do, they do. Then the decision has been made, and I'll be relieved, and can carry on with building homes for people in need.'

By the end of the service I had made my decision. I sought out Fred in the vestry.

'Fred, how would I take the next steps in exploring a vocation?'

'You let me know that you would like to take the next steps. And then I put you in touch with the examining chaplain.'

'Then I guess you'd better do that.'

What changed my mind? I admitted that I needed a community of hope, which I had already done subconsciously by making my way up the stairs to the church in Dean Street.

The onward path was by no means straightforward. If I felt ambivalent at the start, that's nothing to how I felt as the process unrolled. The structure of pre-ordination examination was rigorous. Many interviews, many questions. What brought you here? What is your understanding of God? What can you offer to the church? There were essays to write and books to read, times of prayer and reflection and times of challenge. Through-out all that, which took months – not least because at one point my file was lost and the process had to begin again – there was a subcurrent of silence about matters of human sexuality (the term the church used as a catch-all, but really meaning same-sex love). Conversations, such as they were, maintained a tone of generality.

'There is one other thing. I'm gay.'

'Yes, I know that. And how, would you say, has that affected your faith?'

'In lots of ways. It's given me a sense, which I might not have had otherwise, of being an outsider. I'm very sure that my upbringing, conventional and quite comfortable, would not have led me here had I not been gay.'

'But you're aware of the church's teaching? The expectation that clergy will be celibate?'

'Well, I'm not in a relationship at the moment,' I said. 'And I have no idea whether that will happen in the future' (crossing my fingers behind my back, knowing that my hope, of course, was to meet the man of my dreams ...) 'And, of course, change is always possible within the church.'

In 1991 the formalization of the House of Bishops' position on human sexuality had not yet been completed. So I was not required to sign anything, and it felt usually as if the inter-viewer was glad to move on to less contentious topics, like how I understood the sacrament of Holy Communion. I satisfied my conscience; I was being as open as I could; I moved through the process.

My parents had their doubts. My mother, especially. She was at a loss to understand why I should do this when I had already embarked upon a perfectly satisfactory career, pro-viding housing for people in need. Her doubts were expressed through a stern resistance, a lack of desire to know about what I was doing and who I was meeting. That was fine by me. I had long since stopped trying to tell my mother about my inner being. The ordination process merely became another thing to gloss over when we met.

Eventually, I was called to a selection conference, which took place in an ecclesiastical retreat house in the cathedral close in Chester. A three-day residential conference, eating and social- izing and talking together, a selection panel of six people and 12 or 13 candidates. Beige carpets and wood-pannelled rooms. Plentiful food – spaghetti bolognese and chicken pie, no non- sense about vegetarianism in those days – and chatting lightly over supper. Exercises: a pastoral letter to someone facing a crisis over, as far as I remember, their alcoholic son. One-to- one conversations. My general interview was conducted by a bishop – I forget which, now – and on the table in front of him was my application form. Against my school, and my uni- versity, I saw a large tick. I had the right background.

There was a pastoral interview, which descended quickly into awkwardness. It took place in a small interview room overlooking the walls of Chester, with a man 15 or 20 years older than me. The function of the pastoral interview was to find out whether I was on a reasonably even keel, or whether I was mad or bad.

'Is there anything else you'd like to talk about?' came the question at the end.

'You know I'm gay?' I blurted out.

'There's nothing on your form about that,' the interviewer said. Up to that point he had given the impression of openness, looking me in the eye as he asked his questions: now he with- drew, and no longer met my glance.

'But it's important to me that you know, you are aware.'

'We don't ask about sexuality. You're not in a relationship, are you?'

'No. But I can't make any promises about the future.'

'Well, you understand the church's position, don't you? That's all we need to say, really. I don't need to mention any- thing in your report. Now, tell me about how you like to spend your leisure time.'

That was it. I went back, later, to go over the conversation again. Again there was awkwardness – and, true to form, when the report came, the question of sexual orientation was not mentioned. So the process continued, and I was accepted for training, and onward along the path I marched.

My parents were still unconvinced. To the point where it became difficult. I wanted, at the very least, some affirmation for the route I was taking. It rarely happened. I find a letter I wrote to my mother in December 1991 from my flat in Finsbury Park, when the selection process was nearing its end:

> You're probably right about the Church in some ways; it's certainly a horribly confused and at times malevolent organization and in many ways it is becoming more so. But within it there are places, things and people of inexpressible richness – and now more than ever the world needs spirit, and it's always difficult but should be rewarding to follow a different path.

And I find another, written on 24 July 1992, after I had been approved to move to the next stage:

> Well, I got through. So the next thing is a selection conference in October. But before that I think you deserve an explanation so that (perhaps) you're not *quite* so sure I'm doing the wrong thing … Yes, the Church is a mess, but if people like me don't go into it it'll be in a worse mess. And at the moment, what we need is a bit more spirituality, not less … All over the country there are sometimes very small (Southwark Diocesan Housing Association) and sometimes very large (Coventry Cathedral) institutions and organizations guarding the ramparts against materialism and selfishness, and all the things that have got the world where it is now.
>
> So as I do feel that I'm called to do something away from the structures around career and materialism, it's better to be involved in something that at least tries and sometimes succeeds … It's important for me that you do understand that I'm not being hasty, or escapist, or trying to hide.
>
> Somebody said the other day that the only really good reason to become a priest is if you think you couldn't live with yourself if you didn't … And the main thing is I promise I'll never try to convert you.
>
> Lots and lots of love,
> Giles

My training started in September 1992. As I was still working for the housing association, I elected to train part time, on the Southwark Ordination Course. The course had been set up in the 1970s as a way to bring into the church more priests who did not have tertiary education, but by the time I joined, the students were from a range of backgrounds. We met on Tuesday evenings in the dark post-war church of Christchurch, off Blackfriars Road by the Thames. My cohort, the year of 1992, contained around 15 people from across the traditions of the Church of England and beyond – Pen, who was a Methodist, and Jean and Marion who were from the United Reformed Church. At the beginning of the first session, our tutor, Martin Baddeley, gave us a picture of the globe. Upside down. Australia at the top and the UK at the bottom. Our job, he said, is to make you look at things differently.

The course was intensive, covering a huge range of subjects, including an introduction to ethics, New Testament, Old Testament, community engagement, listening skills, pastoral care and support, and a placement in an institution such as a hospital or prison. We spent seven weekends each year at Wychcroft (often misheard as Witchcraft), a large redbrick farmhouse that had become the diocesan training centre in the Surrey hills.

I developed close and intense friendships with some of my colleagues, especially Pen, who began to bring delicious bread and hummus which she had made that day for us to eat during the break or afterwards, in the King's Head in Roupell Street, on the way back to the station. We were full of hope and enthusiasm, sponges soaking up knowledge and ideas, listening and learning.

Under the counter, the question of sexuality always lurked. Always I was on the defensive, preparing for rejection, but the course tutors were impeccably supportive without ever being explicit about their agreement or otherwise with the C of E's position. Southwark Ordination Course was a place of nourishment, thanks to the loving care of the tutors, Martin, Georgie Bell and Alan Race; I went to Wychcroft so often that it began to feel like home. The nutty, fresh-baked flavour of the Sunday morning breakfast rolls remains with me.

The moment for ordination to the diaconate finally arrived. We lined up in the cathedral in procession, wearing our new black clerical shirts and white albs. The church was full to bursting with friends and family, including my still-ambivalent mother, and my two sisters, one an atheist and the other, at that stage, a strongly traditional evangelical Christian. The signal was given, the golden cross was raised, and the organ struck up with that vibrant anthem by Hubert Parry, 'I was glad, when they said unto me, let us go to the house of the Lord.' I still get goosebumps remembering those opening chords and the sunlight gleaming through the stained-glass windows as the service proceeded. And remembering the feeling of relief; I had made it through to this stage, despite the sharks circling in the waters around me. What was done could not be undone.

The excitement of my new role was rich and delicious. I was placed in North Dulwich, at the parish of St Faith, with a vicar, Stephen Burdett, who was full of laughter and warmth. The parish was on the borders between Camberwell and Dulwich and drew its congregation from across the social and economic spectrum. I soon took on the traditional role of bingo caller to the elderly people of the Sunrise Crescent estate: Legs 11, Key of the Door 21, Downing Street no 10. I took communion to women housebound from intense osteoarthritis and had run-ins with very conservative people about the ordination of women as priests and then bishops.

And there was Leo. The one I thought had been sent by God, for we spoke first in the cathedral and he, like me, was seeking ordination. We both thought our prince had come. He'd gone to Oxford, I to Cambridge. We shared a childish sense of humour and found ourselves falling into one another's arms at summer school in Salisbury cathedral close. Leaping over flowerbeds and playing long and competitive games of table tennis when we should have been writing essays.

When the time came for ordination, by good fortune and because of the good offices of the Diocesan Director of Ordinands, Leo was placed in the adjoining parish to me. We shared a life and we shared excitement, preparing sermons together, recounting our days in the evening, building relationships with younger members of the congregations, many of whom remain friends now. Our congregations were mutually and unstintingly supportive, once they had got used to the idea. Gardening hints and recipes were thrust upon us, and invitations to supper or lunch, and requests to pray for or with ... so although the letter of the church's law was against us, the spirit was moving strongly within and around us. To the point where we felt in some way that it was necessary to model a perfect relationship, which of course created intolerable pressure and undermined the reality that was by no means as strong as the image we were presenting. And so the bifurcation I was to struggle with so much as the years went by began, and was exacerbated month by month.

12

The eight-day drama

2017

As soon as I opened the front door I could see that Francoise was miserable. She stood in the hall, shrugging off her damp coat and draping it across the banister. I invited her into the study where she sat squeezed into the corner of the sofa, while I took my usual place in the comfortable chair beneath the makeshift cross I had made at the diocesan retreat house, two branches of beechwood lashed together. I had hardly seen her for several months, and I rifled through my memory to try to remember where she had been and why she had been absent. Something to do with the north of England swam into my mind, and then she reminded me: she had been working in Liverpool, attached to hospitals as part of her training, and so she had been unable to join us at St John's.

Francoise is slender as a pencil and seems fragile as porcelain. Her father is from Pakistan, her mother from France, and she grew up in England. But the fragility is only apparent. At the end of her studies she took a break and cycled alone the length of Cuba, and later she went to West Africa to work in a local hospital in a rickety town a hundred miles away from anything familiar.

She had not come to talk to me about Cuba, or about West Africa.

'I've been in a hard place,' she said. 'I've been in a place of darkness.' She looked down at the rug, which I'd bought from a man who had set up a fair-trade carpet factory in Kurdistan. But she was not looking at the rug. She was looking into her heart.

'It feels difficult for me to know how I can carry on. It was the girl', she said, 'who they brought in. One afternoon. Her parents brought her to A & E. She had a headache, they told us, and it wasn't going away.'

'What age was she?'

'She was nine. She hardly spoke: her eyes were half-closed and she looked worn out. Her parents said they just thought they should bring her in to make sure she's OK. We found her a bed. The consultant was working on another emergency. When she was free, she came over quickly and looked at the little girl.'

She stopped again, and her eyes filled with tears. She looked up at me through her glasses, skin clear as a newborn's.

'Three hours later she was dead. Meningitis.'

She stopped talking. I was fond of Francoise: her unexpected laugh, her seriousness, her refusal to take faith for granted and yet not give up on it. I had never seen her so vulnerable. I felt that whatever I could say would seem banal.

'I'm so sorry. I can imagine how you must have felt. I'm sure you did what you could.'

Hopeless, really, just filling the gap.

'I felt – I felt broken,' she said. 'Her parents. They were distraught. You can imagine. They brought a child in, they needed our help, and three hours later the child was a corpse. There was nothing anyone could say. I felt – I felt as though God was not there. There was only grief.'

I realized that the death of the child had sparked something deep within Francoise.

'You were there for them,' I said. 'Meningitis is a most terrible thing. It takes children away so easily, and with no warning.'

'Exactly,' she said. 'And how on earth, why on earth, does God allow that to happen?'

I thought of the great debate between Alexei Karamazov and his brother in Dostoevsky's novel. Ivan Karamazov's contention that there is absolutely nothing, anywhere, that can justify the suffering of an innocent child. Here was Francoise, in my study, asking me for an explanation, for something to make sense of the pain and the grief she was feeling. I could think of nothing to say that could be of any use.

* * * * *

We gathered at St Andrew's, the smaller, newer church for which I am responsible, nearly opposite the Young Vic theatre. Thirty people were there when I arrived with the servers team. I was wearing a red chasuble and stole. Red, for Palm Sunday: the colour for Holy Week is red all the way up to Maundy Thursday, when we burst into white for the celebration of the final feast.

We looked smart in red. We handed out palm crosses, and invited everyone to raise them so that they could be blessed. I reminded the congregation of what I said every year: that we, for the coming week, are reliving one of the most important stories in history, the story of the death and resurrection of Jesus. Whatever actually happened – as Pilate says in St John's Gospel, 'What is truth?' – the story has been told and retold down the centuries by millions upon millions of people, millions upon millions of times: and we are, in Waterloo, part of that retelling. The Holy Week liturgies are the most dramatic of the year. We touch the heights and plumb the depths. We become for a week the disciples and the apostles and the women of Jerusalem. This story of the past has a present life. It is both a recollection and a resurrection. A re-creation. Each time it is told, it is new.

The more you put in, I say, the more you get out. Tom and Jess and Lucia and Deborah and Shanon and Rebecca and a motley of others held high their palms for blessing, and with delight we went forth singing, 'Mine eyes have seen the glory of the coming of the Lord'.

We followed the cross in procession, out into Short Street and along the Cut, and then right at the Old Vic, into Waterloo Road, singing and singing. 'We are marching in the light of God, we are marching in the light of God.' A few tourists took photographs. We felt a little bit daft and a little bit defiant. Walking past Tesco's and Sainsbury's on the Waterloo Road, and under the railway bridge, the singing sounded stronger; it echoed, and the people were pleased.

When we reached St John's we found the doors shut. I lifted the processional cross and knocked with its base three times.

Who is this that seeks entry into Jerusalem?
It is the King of Kings![14]

A moment of nervousness, because sometimes the doorkeepers fail to open the doors at the right moment. This time Ken did the trick, the doors swung open and in we poured, singing merrily:

All glory, laud and honour to thee Redeemer, King,
to whom the lips of children make sweet hosannas ring.[15]

I pitched the tune too high, and Michaiah the organist started lower, so there was confusion and disharmony until people decided to follow the organ and not me ... thus we arrived, tired already from too much singing, and took our places, and the service continued.

We had been disciples, and now we became worshippers. The colour, the tonality of the service changed. The story really was retold, for we had the dramatized reading of the Passion story in the Gospel of Mark. Different people took the parts of Jesus, Pilate, the apostle Peter, Judas, the maid by the fire who accused Peter before his betrayal. Issy and Bena, the twins, took the parts of Jesus and the maid. Mark was narrator. Shanon was, as ever, the maid and played his part with gusto. I filled in, and was the centurion (Awe, truly this man was the Son of God). We lined up along the altar step, clutching our scripts:

PILATE	Then what do you wish me to do with the man you call the King of the Jews?
NARRATOR	They shouted back,
CROWD	Crucify him!
NARRATOR	Pilate asked them,
PILATE	Why, what evil has he done?
NARRATOR	But they shouted all the more,
CROWD	Crucify him! Crucify him!

The congregation joined in. 'Crucify him! Crucify him!' I felt anger in the church, and shame, and a sense of responsibility, and fear.

Holy Week is a raw week. Emotions are close to the surface. And as it is so counterintuitive – longer than a Test Match, much longer than the *Ring* cycle, a passion play in seven acts, taking place quietly and without fanfare in the middle of London, surrounded by people going to work and going out to play – it feels even more strange. We pass into a different time and space. We find ourselves stretched between the now and the infinite. It is like, but not like, listening to a symphony, for we are all participating. It is like, but not like, dreaming, for we are awake. It is a tender privilege, to be part of the Holy Week observances.

13

Unwelcome visit

A warm spring morning; Friday. Leo and I were enjoying our day off, having a slow breakfast in the house the church provided for me in Herne Hill, South London. The bacon was crispy and the eggs perfectly fried. Mushrooms and tomato ketchup and mustard.

The doorbell rang, and I opened the door to find Steve, the curate of the parish next door.

'Steve! A nice surprise. What can we do for you?'

'Can I come in?'

'Of course.' I did not know him well, but we had met at deanery meetings. I knew that he was of a conservative bent, theologically; the Herne Hill parish was strongly evangelical.

'Coffee? As you can see, we're having our breakfast.'

'No coffee, thank you.' He seemed nervous.

'The last time we met was at Deanery Chapter, wasn't it. Have you come to talk about that?' I asked.

'No. I've come to tell you that I do not agree with your lifestyle. I cannot support your living together, you and Leo. I have to say that you are behaving in a way that is sinful.'

Leo and I glanced at each other. We were so taken aback we found it difficult to respond. Steve stood up. I found myself being inexplicably kind, almost to the point of thanking him for coming.

'I understand,' I said. 'But I do hope your view about our relationship won't stop us from working together.'

'I will pray for you both,' he said.

'Let me see you out,' I said, still trying to be pleasant. 'I'm sure we'll meet again soon.' The door closed behind him, and back in the deep blue living room, I found Leo sitting on the sofa. He looked up at me, shock in his eyes.

'Bloody hell.'

'I know,' I said. 'I can't believe that just happened.'

'You know what he was doing?' said Leo. 'He was bearing witness. He was clearing his conscience; following that verse in one of Paul's letters where Paul tells the elders to tell sinners of their sin, so that their conscience is clear and they have warned the sinner of the wickedness of their behaviour.'

'And he came into our house to do that.'

'What can have brought that on?' said Leo.

'No idea. Maybe it was something I said at Chapter. I know the subject came up. It feels horrible, but I'm angry too. What gives him the right to come in like that – and on our day off as well …' Leo laughed, but he looked upset. We hugged, silent for a moment.

'That was shit,' he said. 'I feel raw.'

'Let's go out,' I said. 'We can go to the woods.'

A couple of days later my phone rang.

'Giles? Douglas Bartles-Smith here.'

'Archdeacon! Hello. What can I do for you?'

'I'm just wondering if you and Leo are at home, and if you'd like to pop round for a quick chat.'

I liked Douglas. I'd known him for about three years, since my time as Director of the Southwark Diocesan Housing Association. He could appear gruff on the surface, but his awkwardness masked a deep commitment to social justice and a powerful belief in a gospel of welcome for all.

'Sure, we'll come up on our bikes.'

We rode through the dark and arrived at Dog Kennel Hill at about 9 p.m. We tethered the bikes outside.

'Come in.' He showed us into his study, full of books, an old sofa, a wide desk covered in papers. 'Whisky?' He had prepared the bottle and three glasses. 'Ice or water?' Famous Grouse sploshed liberally into tumblers. He seemed ill at ease.

'Thanks for coming across. You see, I've had a complaint.'

'From Steve?'

'Yes, from Steve. He's asked me to take action, because, he says, you two are living in sin and setting a bad example to your congregations.'

'That's not what our congregations say!' said Leo. 'And we were touched and grateful that the diocese managed to find us parishes next to each other!'

'Yes, I know,' said Douglas. 'And we were pleased too. But the fact remains that you are not married – and I very much doubt that same-sex marriage will ever be possible in the church – and so you are, technically, living in sin and in contravention of the church's discipline.'

'How do you know?' I said. 'We could just be friends.'

'But you're not, are you?' he said. 'Look, you know we want to support you both. You're doing good work as curates and you bring a lot to the deanery. But I've had a chat with the Bishop. He just wondered – he said – well, asked, really – can't you stay a bit more below the radar? I mean, do you have to sleep together *every* night?' As he spoke he topped up our drinks. That's when I began to feel really tired.

'We're just doing the best we can,' said Leo. 'Why shouldn't we sleep together? We're a couple! And what business is it of Steve whether we do or not?'

'The church has rules,' said Douglas. 'That's the trouble. And the rules aren't likely to change. Situational ethics comes into play – you have to do what's possible.'

'It's exhausting,' I said. 'This endless prying and peering. All we're trying to do is live as well as we can and do the job as well as we can.'

'I know,' said Douglas. 'And it's often hard. But nobody said it's going to be easy.'

2016

'All rise!'

We all rose. The Clerk to the Court entered the church, carrying the mace, a long, heavy piece of cast bronze. He was followed by the Chancellor and the Registrar wearing wigs and black gowns. The mace was placed on the table in front of the Chancellor.

'The court is in session.'

Shanon is fond of saying, as a sociologist of religion, that the Church of England is a state within a state. It has its own parliament (the General Synod), its own civil service (Church House), its own sports teams (the diocesan cricket teams), its own barons (the bishops), its own head of state (the Archbishop of Canterbury, though he would deny that term). It also has its own legal system, named canon law, dating back centuries. The only thing it lacks is an army.

St John's had been laid out like a court. On the right, the petitioners and our barrister, Mr Cain Ormondroyd. On the left, the objectors and their barrister. The Chancellor, Mr Philip Petchey, was the judge. Your honour, we called him. For three full days the proposals for the church were considered. Witnesses were called by the petitioners: the architect, Mr Parry. The archdeacon, Mr Gates. The incumbent, Canon Goddard.

We put our case as well as we possibly could. We explained how the 1951 renovation was not fit for purpose, now. The pulpit and lectern were never used, and blocked the space. The sanctuary was encumbered by steps so that the high altar could not be used on Sundays. The lobby at the west end blocked the spatial relationship between the church and the world. The Lady Chapel and the vestry were unsuccessful spaces that added to the sense of the church being more like a sports hall, disproportionately wide because the balconies that originally filled it were not replaced after the bomb.

Our proposals would, we said, enable us to continue to serve the people of Waterloo for another hundred years, bringing the church up to standard, transforming the crypt, bringing light where there was little light, creating a space for worship and performance that would be among the best in London.

After many hours, Mr Ormondroyd had called all our witnesses, and then it was the turn of the objectors. The hearing was properly adversarial. When I was on the stand, I was asked about the acoustic studies we had commissioned: I tried to flannel in my responses because I knew we were vulnerable.

'Just answer the question, please, Canon Goddard.'

We had a formidable range against us: for the Twentieth Century Society, Dr Powers. For Historic England, Dr Barker. For the London Borough of Lambeth, Mr Black. The Twentieth Century Society mustered its supporters. Gradually they made their case – that this was conceived as a complete ensemble in 1951, a fine example of 1950s' neo-classicism with a particular historical reference to the Festival of Britain. Here at St John's we have at the heart of the building, above the altar, a painting of a crucified man in the last moments of his death, a picture of grief painted by a Jewish refugee who escaped almost certain death at the hands of the Nazis. Hans Feibusch painted this picture as part of the resurrection hope that underlay the Festival. Overall, the workmanship was very fine, the pulpit and lectern represented an essential part of the whole, the sanctuary steps should remain unchanged, the Lady Chapel and the vestry were integral to the structure and should remain unchanged ... In short, all our proposals for the east end were objectionable. There should be no change.

Solemnly the Chancellor listened, enquired, took notes, sought clarification. The people of the parish provided abundant tea and coffee, and sandwiches at lunchtime. It felt like watching a game of croquet played by experts, the tactics unfathomable. Mr Ormondroyd worked hard, listened intently, made his points well: the church was no longer fit for purpose, and for it to flourish there needed to be changes. For everything to stay the same, everything must change. I was tense, cross, resentful. How much was all this costing? And how dare the Twentieth Century Society and the heritage bodies presume to tell us what we could and could not do with our building? Power without responsibility, I thought. Wasting everybody's time and our money. Half my life was being taken up with fundraising – the project was, we thought, at that stage, likely to cost about £3 million. Did they think we were doing it for fun?

I had form on consistory courts. We had proposed changes to the crypt in the last church for which I was responsible, the John Soane church of St Peter's Walworth. There, the Georgian Group objected to the demolition of some of the brickwork.

We had had a court hearing, and Mr George, the Chancellor at the time, had heard the case. We won, and the crypt at St Peter's is now a flourishing community centre called InSpire.

Could I pull it off a second time? After three days, Mr Petchey declared the court closed. The mace was borne back into the Lady Chapel and the lawyers removed their wigs. The parish cleared up the tea and coffee cups and turned the space back into a church, and we waited for the judgement to be handed down.

14

The Triduum

Maundy Thursday rises out of Holy Week like a sun-bright iceberg. The liturgical colour is white. White for celebration, white for humility, white for love. In the midst of the bleakness, an in-breaking of celebration. Lent finished on the Wednesday of Holy Week, and now we move into act five of this seven-act week-long drama. As actors we have to suspend our disbelief and behave as if we do not know how the drama ends.

This act starts well. Friends gather for a meal in an upper room. A group coming together to carry out their long-authenticated ritual, retelling the great story of the Exodus, of the liberation of the people of Israel from slavery in Egypt, at the behest of the religious leader who has transformed their lives.

There have been mutterings about him on the street and in the corridors of power. Who is this man who is challenging our priests and Pharisees, arguing with them in the public square, making them appear stupid and inept? Who is this man who has been popping up around Galilee and in Jerusalem, his motley crowd surrounding him, a bunch of ne'er-do-wells and tax-collectors and fishermen and women – is he dangerous, or is he a crank?

His followers believe he is neither, and they are pleased to be sitting down to relive the Passover meal with him. Usually they would have been with their families, but this year it's clear that Jesus wants them there; no one quite knows why, but no one dares to go home to where their women and children are waiting for them, perhaps keeping a Passover feast of their own, leaving a place at the table for the absent family member.

The meal becomes something very different from anything that those men, and the women silent in the accounts but certainly there, have ever experienced. When Jesus takes off his robe, ties a towel around his waist and kneels at the feet of his followers to wash the dust and dirt off their cracked skin, they are all horrified. Peter, particularly, recoils: no, master, you will not wash my feet! Jesus, quiet as ever, looks into his soul: yes, Peter, I will wash your feet, for if I do not wash yours, then how can I be sure that, when I'm gone, you will wash one another's? In that case, Lord, not just my feet but my hands and my head also. Peter the impulsive, who so often gets it wrong, but once he's realized his mistake has the courage to get it right.

Here at St John's we have developed a tradition that holds the washing of the feet at its heart but remembers too the Jewish heritage of the scriptures. We alternate. The first year, the priests wrap towels around their waists and kneel, washing the feet of the people. It's an extraordinarily moving moment. The chairs are laid out in a short row, and the people come and sit on the chairs and remove their socks and shoes. On each foot I spill a little water and rub a little with my fingers and dry off with the towel and then I move on. I do not have time to look up and see which limbs belong to whom, all I see is a series of feet, some knobbly and misshapen with corns and bunions, some young and slender, some with toes twisted out of shape by rheumatism or arthritis, some athletic and obviously used to being stuck into trainers for a five-a-side football match on the Hatfields pitch. Some brown, some yellow, some white, some black.

It is a uniquely bizarre moment: how often does one wash the feet of anyone else, let alone a stranger's feet? Never, unless they are dead, or wounded. Most of those who come this evening have been kind. They have washed their feet already and put clean socks on; but some haven't, and the intimacy of smells is powerful.

It's a variation of the Sunday ritual, when I go along the row of communicants and place a wafer in each hand. Feet are more intimate, more extraordinary, more of a privilege.

In the alternate years we do something different; we remind ourselves of the Passover tradition. We have a feast. We gather bitter herbs and unleavened bread (matzos) and chopped egg and haroset – Jenny usually makes the haroset, out of a recipe of chopped apples, walnuts, cinnamon, honey – and a table is laid out at the front of church, for 50 or 60 people. I usually roast the legs of lamb and someone else produces the potatoes, and there is much wine and chat, and eventually the youngest person there, usually Oisin, asks the questions:

How is this night different from all other nights?
On all other nights, we eat chameitz and matzah.
   Why on this night, only matzah?
On all other nights, we eat all vegetables.
   Why, on this night, maror?
On all other nights, we don't dip even once.
   Why on this night do we dip twice?

The story is retold. We don't do it all, perhaps impiously, but I have been to Passover meals with Jewish friends and I know that the whole thing, done properly, can take hours, most of the night. There are those who say that to re-create the Passover feast in this way is disrespectful of the rich tradition of Judaism, stretching back millennia, but there are others who acknowledge the power of grounding the story of Holy Week in the rituals out of which Christianity emerged.

Francoise says to me afterwards, 'I had never understood before how deeply rooted we are in the traditions of Judaism.'

'But Jesus was a Jew, wasn't he?'

'Oh yes, I suppose he was. I always forget that.'

The church is dark, the lighting is low, and the murmur of conversation continues. We are a bit squiffy. At last the meal comes to an end, and the people clear their plates and remove the tables, and we gather round the altar in the half-dark and sing the Maundy Thursday hymn:

My song is love unknown –
My Saviour's love to me;
love to the loveless shown,
that they might lovely be.[16]

After I have consecrated the unleavened bread and blessed the
wine, we receive communion. We return to our places and with
great solemnity I am dressed in a humeral veil, a rectangle of
embroidered scarlet cloth. Wrapping my hands in the veil so
that the sacrament is untouched by human hand, I lift the silver
ciborium that contains the body of Christ. I carry it in procession, accompanied by the servers, their candles flickering in the
darkened space, into the garden of Gethsemane. The congregation sing quietly the great hymn written by St Thomas Aquinas:

Of the glorious body telling,
O my tongue, its mysteries sing,
And the blood, all price excelling,
Which the world's eternal King,
In a noble womb once dwelling,
Shed for this world's ransoming.[17]

The garden has been created earlier in the day. The chapel is
filled with yellow primroses, white lilies, sun-touched daffodils
and some early lilac, and the place is heady with the scent of
flowers and warm with the amber light of candles. We bear the
sacrament in and place it on the altar.

The service ends, and afterwards people come to sit in the
garden, and some of them are tired and tipsy, as I am, and
as I watch them and watch the candles burning down and try
to pray I am conscious of eyelids closing, and I remember the
story, of the disciples in the garden of Gethsemane, 'Could you
not wait with me, even so long?' Of course, they'd had enough
to drink too. No wonder they went to sleep.

As we walk home, at 11 o'clock on a Thursday night, the
streets are alive and drunk people are running to catch their
trains from Waterloo and an ambulance goes past, siren screech-
ing, and it all feels very distant. Yet these are the people whose

feet I am called to wash, too, and I am glad that outside of the circle of drama we are creating, the life of the city rushes on.

Something happens as we enter the Triduum, these last three days of the great drama. I move into a different space. The squabbles and the anxieties and the horrors of the church are parked somewhere beyond the city walls of Jerusalem. I am caught up in the deeply human story of fear, betrayal, condemnation and summary execution. I suspend my anger and my resentment at the church, and with the people of St John's I try to play my part.

During these days I am especially aware of the strata of history and tradition stretching beneath us, a ragged bunch living out our lives on a marsh that will in time be compressed into another layer of soil. My hopes, my fears, my desires will fall like dead leaves to join the detritus of time. Others will come to live where I live now. But the echo of the curlew's call will still sound through Waterloo, and I hope the story of Holy Week will still be told.

1998

Holy Week's mix of emptiness, action and death makes me think of my father: in particular, his death in 1998.

I was in the third year of my curacy in the parish in North Dulwich, learning the job, struggling to keep the relationship with Leo going, struggling to reconcile the bifurcations in my life, presenting a public face of warmth and enthusiasm: 'That Giles, he's a nice young priest.'

My father had been unwell for a few weeks. No one was sure why. Tests were done. His blood sugar levels were all over the place. He lacked energy. He had unexplained pains in his body.

He and my mother were living in North Oxfordshire. The house was full of my mother's anger. My father was a good person but unsuccessful in business. He had gone into partnership with a man who had a lamp-making company in Cheshire, producing ceramic lamp bases for sale in shops like John Lewis and Selfridges. It seemed like a sound company and the man was convincing; my father wanted to make a success of his retirement, and he decided it would be good to invest in the lamp-making company and help it to thrive so that he and my mother could retire on a healthy pension.

But the timing was wrong. A recession was round the corner, and the man turned out to be a charlatan, and my father, unwilling to admit that he had made a wrong decision, threw good money after bad, and then threw my mother's money in too, without asking her. The firm went bankrupt, and one morning at 5 a.m. the police rang the doorbell. They took shed-loads of files away, and then a letter arrived from the Crown Prosecution Service telling my father that he, as a co-director, was under suspicion of trading while knowingly insolvent, for which the maximum sentence is a term in jail.

The charlatan did go to jail. My father was forbidden from being a director again. This last failure diminished him and exponentially increased my mother's anger.

Like many others seeking solace, he followed up his family tree in even greater depth. He took photographs too, lots of photographs, and stuck them in big albums, many bright pictures of flowers and trees. He enjoyed the garden, a bramley apple tree honourably standing in the centre. He drank, in sometimes moderate and sometimes less moderate quantities. And still, though unseen by me, he nourished an immense love for the world and for the people around him, and despite everything he stayed loyal to my mother, who even then, towards the end of their lives together, was unable to overcome the bitterness that had gnawed at her for so many years.

Their relationship became even more complex when she and he had to work out how to live a new regime, that of a diabetic, a new attempt to explain why his sugar levels were weirdly unstable. Nothing they did seemed to help. He returned to hospital, and more tests were done, and after a few days we were called in by the consultant who advised us that advanced cancer had been found in the pancreas, and that we could expect him to live for, perhaps, another year.

Gay Pride was in Brixton that year. Leo and I went, for it was just down the road. There was a fashion for extra-strong lager.

We drank two, or maybe three, or perhaps four, and danced till dark, and walked home. We were scarcely able to stand up. The phone was ringing as we stumbled through the door.

'Giles, the hospital have rung. They think we should go in, first thing tomorrow.'

'OK,' I slurred. 'I'll come down in the morning.'

The phone woke me again at 5 a.m.

'Giles, the hospital rang. We should go in now.'

'OK. I'm on my way.'

I went to the bathroom, peered in the mirror. I found I had a huge black eye and no memory of how I had got it. Back in the bedroom I found the door handle broken on the floor. I must have bashed the door in an early morning trip to the loo. No matter, I had to get to Banbury. The motorbike was in Bermondsey, where Leo was living. I realized that I did not want to be present at my father's death: that I wanted to arrive long afterwards. I dawdled. I told myself I need to sober up. I had toast for breakfast. I felt curiously cold and calm, and afraid of having to express emotions I was not able to express. I caught the bus to Bermondsey and then drove the bike down through a nearly empty London and up the M40, not rushing, towards the hospital. I arrived at 9 p.m. to find my mother and my sister waiting for me outside the main door. Mum looked at me, not sure where to start.

'What on earth has happened to your eye? Your father's gone, he's inside, you can see him if you like. Why have you taken so long? Where have you been?'

I said nothing. I was taken to the ward. There, behind a curtain (the hospital had not had time to move him to a side ward), was my father. Yellow from jaundice induced by the failure of the pancreas, and waxy, and very dead.

His funeral was extraordinary. The church was crammed. The words of praise and sadness were overwhelming. Letters arrived too, dozens of letters. Over and over again people spoke of his thoughtfulness, his care, his generosity, his humour. The attention he gave to the people he was speaking with. His interest in others. I received a picture of a man I barely knew, had barely tried to get to know.

After the funeral, I began to find sleep hard. I spent long dark nights of the soul, awake and unhappy. By day, I had a series of masks, of constructed selves. I moved to a new church to become rector – St Peter's, in Walworth, between Elephant and Castle and Camberwell. The church flourished. I was busy and engaged in the local community. I was much loved. I was careful and thoughtful and competent. Or I was a sex-fiend in a backroom, taking precautions, of course, in these post-AIDS days, but playing the field like a premier league star. Or I was a loyal friend to those around me. Or I was a sophisticated Londoner. Or I was a spiritual pilgrim, fervently seeking enlightenment through the words and example of St Francis and Jesus. Or I was grieving a father I hardly knew and a brother who died long before I was born.

Outwardly, I played the parts I was given, offering these incompatible selves to the world around me. Inwardly, I had not yet understood that the one thing I was not was Giles Goddard.

2017

An email dropped into my inbox in February 2017, from the diocesan registrar: 'Dear Canon Goddard, please find attached the Chancellor's judgement in respect of your Petition for Faculty for works at St John's Church, Waterloo.'

I was rushing from one meeting to another and tried to open the email on my phone. The judgement was in a pdf. I tried to flick through to get the result. It was 60 pages long and on a phone such a document is hard to read. I realized I had to stop and to give this thing my full attention. I sat down and opened my laptop, and downloaded the judgement again.

IN THE CONSISTORY COURT OF THE DIOCESE OF SOUTHWARK IN THE MATTER OF ST JOHN'S CHURCH, WATERLOO, AND IN THE MATTER OF A PETITION BY THE REVEREND CANON GILES GODDARD, MRS BELINDA TAYLOR AND MR DAVID CLARSON.

Anxiously I scrolled through the pages. Introduction. The background facts. The Parish. The Church. The Proposals. The

History. Statement of Need. Statement of Significance. Letters of Support (there is a letter from Baroness Wheeler of Blackfriars ... Baroness Wheeler is Chair of the Blackfriars Settlement. She says, 'The project has the full support and enthusiasm of the local community'). The National Planning Policy Framework. All that and I was still only at page 27, and I still had no idea whether our application has been granted or refused.

In great detail, carefully considering, the Chancellor set out the legal arguments. He looked at former cases. He outlined the evidence he had heard, and noted the arguments of Mr Pike and Mr Ormondroyd.

Anxiously I scrolled on. Substantial harm. There was substantial harm. But was there public benefit? And did the public benefit outweigh the harm? Hurriedly I read, the words swimming, my heart pattering. I read all the way through to the end and still could not see the decision. I was expecting a statement, like a BBC1 game show: the prize is yours! Or: you are the weakest link. Goodbye.

I reread the final pages. Finally I lit upon paragraph 269:

269 (5) Bearing in mind that there is a strong presumption against proposals that will adversely affect the special character of a listed building, will any resulting public benefit (including matters such as liturgical freedom, pastoral well-being and putting the church to viable uses that are consistent with its role as a place of worship) outweigh the harm? In answering question (5), the more serious the harm, the greater the public benefit needed before the proposals should be permitted. This will particularly be the case if the harm is to a building that is listed Grade I or II*, where serious harm should only exceptionally be allowed.

270 I have formed the view that, for the reasons I have given, an exception should not be made in the present case.

I read and reread that sentence. My heart crashed through the floor. All that work, all that time, all that money, all those people's commitment and effort – and our application had been refused. A very public failure – the wider church's eyes upon us: 'Oh, Giles, he'll be OK, he always gets things done!' Not this time. Part of me wanted to crawl into the cellar and not tell anyone. I closed my laptop, picked up my keys and went down to the river where I leant on the railing and watched the tour boats go back and forth, and watched the brown tide rush out, and wondered how I was going to break the news to the parish. I prayed, urgently, and reflected, urgently, on how we had got to this situation. I was afraid; it felt as if we were going to be stuck with the space as it was, for ever. Perhaps I should give up on trying to improve it.

2018

On Good Friday, darkness dawns. There is little to say about this day that hasn't already been said, and yet every year it is new. The emptiness that we left behind in the darkened church is still there. The sanctuary light gutters next to the sacrament in the chapel, but it gutters alone, and, where there should be a mass of silver candlesticks and brass crosses and bright hangings, on the altar is only an expanse of empty floor, for we stripped the altars on Maundy Thursday.

The ladies of the parish arrived. The (cold) hot cross buns were as yet unbuttered. We sat quietly, a production line: I cut, Heather buttered, Eileen placed them on the tray for later. Holly was there too – she struggled in, she got a taxi, and on this day of purple and black her garb was even more appropriate.

'Come on in, darlings!' she called as she buttered, and a few people drifted in, some from the Catholic church behind my house. We greeted them, friends who we see once a year on this dark day, and together we set off behind the cross, singing feebly in the streets behind the church,

When I survey the wondrous cross
on which the Prince of glory died,
my richest gain I count but loss,
and pour contempt on all my pride.[18]

One year, perhaps 2018, I was obsessed by Schubert's piano sonatas. It felt as if I listened to nothing else that Lent. There are particular sonatas I chose for particular times, and some I saved for special occasions, perhaps particularly reflective or joyful or heartbroken. Schubert takes me on a journey with each one, leads me along unexpected paths, the structure by no means as clear or as comprehensible as Beethoven's majestic works, or as carefully planned as Brahms'. He had trouble with sonatas. He started at least 21 but only completed 11.

D784 in A minor, number 14, was for Good Friday. The first movement especially. The theme stated quietly, a lonely theme, a whispered cry for help in the middle of the storm, Jesus alone in the high priest's house awaiting his summary sentence, the music working out the story, taking us into anguish and tranquillity: 'My God, my God, why have you forsaken me?', 'Father, forgive them; for they do not know what they are doing.' I listened to it in the interval between the walk of witness and the Good Friday liturgy.

The day is shaded by the liturgical colour: black or purple. Our curate Lisa and I enter the church at 1.30 p.m. from the vestry, wearing our black cassocks; we prostrate ourselves in the empty sanctuary, while those around us sit silent. We lie outstretched on the floor and I feel the cold of the stones creeping up through my garments. When I judge the moment right I stand up, and Lisa stands alongside me, and the congregation stands, and I read the Collect for Good Friday.

In silence we all go to the back of the church, and Andy lifts the cross, the wooden cross, the rough cross that was carried in the morning around the parish, and bears it heavily up towards the sanctuary. Three times, we stop.

This is the wood of the cross,
on which hung the Saviour of the world.
O come, let us worship.[19]

The day is a massive contradiction. How can we hold up the instrument of torture, of the death of Jesus, as anything other than purely, lightlessly, evil? It's a conundrum, even greater when we reach the ancient ceremony of the veneration of the cross; when the more observant or the more ritualistic of us genuflect before the cross where it lies alone in the sanctuary. Some kiss it. The first time I saw that I was shocked, these heights of Catholic ritual, certainly idolatrous. But now it seems to make sense: an acknowledgement of the reality of evil, of our own destructive actions, our pride, our arrogance, our will to power – and of our societies' destructive actions too, the oppression of the weak, the exploitation of the poor, the ravaging of the natural world, climate breakdown. As it says in Psalm 123.4:

> Our soul has had more than its fill
> of the scorn of those who are at ease,
> of the contempt of the proud.

Something deeper than that. Embracing the wound. The cross is the symbol of hope because it speaks of the divine entering into the reality of human destructiveness – what Francis Spufford calls 'the human propensity to fuck things up'.[20] The Good Friday liturgy incorporates sin into the story and, by naming and apparently submitting to it, removes its power.

How can we escape the downward spiral of destruction? How can we live in hope when hope is in short supply, perhaps non-existent? How can we change the heartbreaking story of sonata no 14 in A minor?

We don't. The cross does.

So we kiss it, one by one, sincerely, awkwardly.

Awkwardness gives way to heartbreak as the service reaches its conclusion. I bring the sacrament from the chapel, in a workaday manner, without procession. I take the bread from person to person, and each person eats a piece, and in the end there is none left.

The sacrament is gone. The body of Christ is exhausted. Christ is dead. The lamp that was guttering in the sanctuary is blown out, and the dead candle with the after-smoke curling into the sunlight is placed on the ground next to the cross. One by one we stand and leave the building, until I, last out, close the front doors and switch on the alarm and depart by the side door, which I lock behind me. The church is no longer a church. It is a void surrounded by walls.

1998

The twisted dynamics continued. My relationship with Leo, unable to bear the pressures upon it, came to a difficult and painful end. My head played games with my heart, and I carried on in a way that was both exploitative and harsh, and as a result many people got hurt who should not have been, over the next 20 years.

The bifurcation became complete. I had a public life and a private life, and although I believed I had brought them together I was fooling myself. The lives I was living became more divided. More casual sex and more illegal drugs, to the point where my life was sometimes at risk, and my reputation often.

There were moments of joy – moments that felt transcendent, in the dark, with the lights swirling and the music shining – moments when I knew God was present on the dance floor. The Chemical Brothers sang 'God is a DJ', and I was in their church that night, knowing that 'this is where I heal my hurts.'[21] The bass burrowed into me and my shirt came off and my arms went up. The beat and the universe and the dancers and I were merged. We became one. Time had no meaning.

Looking back I can see now how lucky I was that, no matter how close to the edge I danced, I never spun over the cliff. There came a night when I thought I was about to die from over-consumption of some powder or other. We called the ambulance, but I held on to enough sanity to realize that an ambulance would be the end of everything, and in my haze I managed to convince them that they should not come. The line between tragedy and survival was wafer thin, and I wonder now that I am alive to tell the tale.

2018

There is no colour for Holy Saturday. There is nothing. The tabernacle is open and the candle that burns beside it throughout the year is extinguished. The sanctuary is empty. There are marks on the floor where the altar should be, and the place echoes even more than usual.

It reminds me of Saturdays at school, after lessons finish at 1 p.m., and nearly everyone has gone back to their homes for the weekend. The cloisters are empty. I hear the footsteps of another boy descending the steps on the far side of the quad but I can't see who it is. The sky is flat and overcast, darkening the grey flint walls to a shade of black. I cannot go home this weekend, or perhaps I choose not to, because home does not feel like home, it is as much a place of sadness as school.

I go down to the music school, hoping that Charlie may be there. Charlie is the focus of all my intensity at the moment. He plays the oboe with great skill. He plays the piano too: he can harmonize and vamp and build a wall of loveliness, or he can make the oboe weep filaments of loneliness. He knows I am in love with him, but nothing is said and nothing happens, except that I hang around the music school like a piece of driftwood hoping that Charlie will be there.

He isn't. And Bruce is not in his houseroom, and Bernhard is writing an essay and cannot be disturbed. I wander out of the school buildings and up the avenue of poplars towards the open-air theatre, bare and desolate on this late winter afternoon, and from there on to the emptiness of the South Downs. I pick my way over chalk stones in the path, alongside the rusting barbed-wire fence where early spring wheat lightens the dark earth with a breath of green. I wish I could have gone home but home is as lonely as school. Neither here or there do I have any sense of who or what I am, except that I am sure that whatever it is must be something contemptible.

On Holy Saturday time stops. Jesus is dead. God's fatherhood is destroyed by human depravity. There is, on Holy Saturday, no corridor between the temporal and eternal. We are truly on our own, a dirty tennis ball kicked through the cosmos.

When Judas, his betrayer, saw that Jesus was condemned, he repented and brought back the thirty pieces of silver to the chief priests and the elders. He said, 'I have sinned by betraying innocent blood.' But they said, 'What is that to us? See to it yourself.' Throwing down the pieces of silver in the temple, he departed; and he went and hanged himself. (Matt. 27.3–5)

The seafarer is out on the cold sea, hearing the call of the curlew and grieving the fellowship of the city. He is far from the comforts of his home, the companionship and the security. He has voyaged across windswept wastes in his tiny, fragile ship, the ropes creaking as the mast bends under the weight of the sails. He wonders why he has left his home; he knows he is under the finger of fate; but he also knows that the journey is a journey he has to take.

PART 4

Easter to Christ the King

15

Waterloo sunrise

2018

At 4.45 a.m. the alarm drags us out of sleep. It's hand-flapping dark and the room is cold. I swear and hit the snooze button.

'We have to get up,' mutters Shanon.

'Why? I don't want to go to church.'

'You have to. You're the vicar.'

Grumbling, I haul myself into the shower, hurrying now, not wanting to be late. That half-conscious feeling of very early awakening, the world through a piece of gauze.

Walking across to St Andrew's in the cold dark of a very early spring morning is a delight. A blackbird high in a cherry tree whistles at us, piercing the thin quiet before dawn. When we arrive at St Andrew's we are greeted by the assembled company looking smug because they were there first. There are too many lights on in the church. I turn some off. I'm always grumpy before the service starts.

On Holy Saturday we got the church ready. We dug rags and dusters from the back of the safe. We polished the brass and arranged the flowers and cleaned the candlesticks and restored the sanctuary. Afterwards Ken and Eileen came over to St Andrew's and Ken found some pieces of kindling and some newspaper and created the brazier for the morning.

On Easter Day, while it is still dark, I put on my alb and my white stole – we leave purple and black behind on this day of high festival – and I go outside carrying the Paschal candle, as heavy as a baby and twice as long, and I am greeted by the assembled crowd: 20 brave people who have set the alarm for ridiculously early and are gathered in their coats and mufflers outside the church, waiting for the ritual to begin.

The dawn Mass – the great Liturgy of Easter. Many churches hold it on the Saturday evening but that seems lightweight to me. Let the austerity continue for a few more hours. Then let everyone stand outside in the cold dawn, to hear again the story of liberation that we are about to celebrate.

'There should be some element of waiting,' say the rubrics in *Common Worship*. 'Personal, historical and biblical stories of escape might be shared.' My friend Tim lives on a beach in Suffolk, and there the people gather on the shingle by the sound of the waves. We have no sea in Waterloo, not any more, but sometimes we are blessed by drops of chilling rain as we stand to hear again the great story of the Exodus. And the wonderful image of the dry bones in the book of the prophet Ezekiel. In my last church I always asked Doreen to read the Ezekiel reading, for her Barbadian accent lifted all our hearts:

[The LORD] said to me, 'Mortal, can these bones live? I answered, 'O Lord GOD, you know.' Then he said to me, 'Prophesy to these bones …'

So I prophesied as I had been commanded; and as I prophesied, suddenly there was a noise, a rattling, and the bones came together, bone to its bone.' (Ezek. 37.3–4, 7)

The readings go on, and on, and on, and by the end people are shivering. After we have heard all five readings I say a prayer, and I take the lighter from Ken, and I lean down and set a light to the edge of the paper. It has been pre-primed with something unconscionable, and quickly the flames lick the kindling and the brazier bursts into fire and there is a beacon in the darkness, a warmth of gold lighting the faces of the congregation, and they smile in the dawn. I take the candle, and struggle with the taper, because the flames are so hot now that I cannot get near them to bring out a flame to light the candle, and everyone laughs and the taper melts. But in the end there is a flame that I lift to the wick, and the candle is lit, and luckily it is a breathless morning, so when I hand the candle to Lisa to carry in, she holds it high as she walks from the street into the darkened church, and the light shines in the darkness.

'The Light of Christ,' she sings. 'Thanks be to God,' we respond.

The candle is carried in a little further and we shuffle behind.

'The Light of Christ,' she sings, a tone higher. 'Thanks be to God!'

The candle is placed in its stand, in the darkness.

'The Light of Christ!' a tone higher. 'Thanks be to God!'

The congregation is holding candles. I take one, and light it from the Paschal candle, and pass the light around, and the church begins to glow, and people's faces are glimmering and warm as they stand around the candle in a semi-circle. Lisa draws in her breath and begins the great hymn of Easter, its music stretching back to the fourth or fifth century, the allocating of this role to young recently ordained deacons such cruelty, this long piece that curls and twists and wanders, unaccompanied plainsong, difficult and beautiful and resonating through the candlelit church:

Rejoice, heavenly powers!
Sing, choirs of angels!
Exalt, all creation around God's throne!
Jesus Christ our King is risen![22]

It is the highlight of the year, this ancient ritual of fire and water. Later in the service we go outside again, to the tiny courtyard wherein stands an olive tree and a font. Bearing the candle, we plunge it into the water:

'Springs of water, bless the Lord!'

and the congregation renews its baptismal vows:

'We believe in God the Father Almighty, who created the
heavens and the earth!'

I sprinkle them all with this newly blessed water in the newly risen light of Christ, and we are whole and we are joyful.

Or, we are a group of middle-aged people and pensioners a

little surprised at ourselves, squeezed into a courtyard as the dawn comes up. But perhaps it has always been thus, even in the fourth or fifth century when these liturgies were first developed, when baptisms only happened on Easter morning, when the harshness of winter was infinitely greater than it is now and the first green shoots of spring emerging would have resonated epically with the retelling of the resurrection story.

Liturgy derives from the Greek *leitos* (public) and *ergos* (work). It is, literally, the work of the people, and the people are you and me. I am alongside the people I have journeyed with through Lent, alongside Alice and Shanon and Francoise and Ida and Holly and Matthew and Alice, and once we have shared in the first communion of Easter the room is cleared, and tables appear, and Eileen magics up cornflakes and boiled eggs and marmite and honey and jam and coffee and tea and toast, and the obligatory accompaniment to Easter breakfast: champagne.

The buzz of fizz on an empty stomach at seven o'clock on Easter Sunday morning. It's a delight. I recommend it.

16

Wisdom of centuries

There is a wise tradition in Christianity. People are often recommended to have a spiritual director – a soul friend – someone who can walk alongside them as they seek to understand more fully the truths they are trying to discover. Someone who can listen to their questions and nudge them gently in a different direction. In the past the person was often also their confessor, someone to hear their sins and absolve them, but that is rare now.

Ten years after I became a priest, five years after the death of my father, I realized that I felt dried up, spiritually and mentally. Worship and prayer were feeling like pointless gestures and empty words.

The sense of being an insider outside, or an outsider inside. My place in my family unassured. I felt my mother's love to be conditional, at best. The death of my father simplified the relationship, potentially, but we found it hard to communicate. She took against the boyfriends I introduced her to.

'You're such a bad picker, Giles. They just want to use you.'

Always a disappointment, and yet always the one she relied on most of the three of us. After my father's death, bereavement counsellors came to her house.

'I sent them away,' she told me. 'I said to them, "What on earth are you thinking?" I wasn't going to be taken apart and then put back together again!'

Betwixt and between, somehow lost in no man's land. I was desperate to find love, but at the same time I went often to the Vauxhall Tavern and did things that were not good for my body or my soul. My emotional coldness was mirrored, I thought, in others. I went in deep, and then withdrew quickly as soon as I decided that I'd made a mistake. I expected them to be able to bounce back as quickly as I did. I justified it through a sort of cod-existentialism – that it was always better to live than not to live. The trouble was, living was not really living, and my actions were acts: whereas for those around me, the actions had meaning and the hurt I caused was real.

A recommendation led me to Julie, a wise and thoughtful woman from the United States about my age. She had spent much of her life exploring the spiritual journey with the help of many, the ascetic Ignatius of Loyola, the poet Mary Oliver, the infinitely serious and generous Richard Rohr, and many more. We met in a little unwindowed room at the church of St Edmund in the City, and there she began to unravel the knotted threads that were tangled round my heart.

'The problem is', I said, 'that I am trying to live the life of a priest and the life of a London gay man.' I held my arms out as wide as I could. 'And this is how far apart they feel.'

She warned me not to expect instant miracles. For I still had the need for love. I was unable to believe that I was loved and loveable. I needed to learn that loving other people is not about power and influence and holding sway. It is about allowing the other, whoever they might be, to flourish. Something I had often repeated in church. But did I believe what I said in church? No. I surrounded myself with weapons of self-protection.

Julie is a gifted listener, someone who can take a simple phrase and unlock it, allowing its implications to resonate. Often we talked of the need for nourishment, for depth of soil, for the shoots to grow, to take root. My spiritual life was shallow, at that stage. Attendance at daily prayer and worship was, I thought, enough. But Julie had other ideas, and I could not escape the tug of the divine, and slowly she gave me the confidence to trust the growth of my spiritual life.

The process was not simple or straightforward. Julie walked alongside me, listening and reflecting, and encouraging me more deeply into prayer. She recommended, especially, silent meditation. Christian meditation – the rediscovery of an ancient Christian tradition of repeating a mantra, silently, for a set time every day, perhaps 20 minutes, perhaps more.

I worked out my own mantra and began to set my alarm for a little earlier each morning. I sat in a chair and opened my heart with a version of the great prayer of St Augustine.

> Almighty God, you made us for yourself and our hearts are restless till they find their rest in you. Pour into our hearts such love towards you that we, loving you above all things, may receive all your promises for us, which exceed all that we can either desire or deserve, through Jesus Christ, your Son, our Lord, Amen.[23]

And then I repeated, silently, under my breath:

> Bless the Lord, O my soul, O bless the Lord.

Simple, and effective. Gradually. There was no sudden leap into freedom. But there was after a while a quiet sense that something was changing. A feeling as if the tectonic plates within me were starting to realign, inch by inch, so that they fit more closely together. The ground became firmer under my feet. The path began to become clearer.

I burrowed into the wisdom of many before me who feared the fears I confront and held the hopes I hold: John of the Cross, Mother Julian of Norwich, Rumi; ordinary people who have changed the world. A hunger for spiritual fulfilment, lived out in ways exceptional but not unique. The hunger for a rich spirituality is ubiquitous. The desire for the light of life touches men and women everywhere. Even in Waterloo.

2018

Resurrection. It begins with the personal. It begins with my own personal awareness of my own personal darkness. He descended into hell.

Throughout a particular Holy Week, 2018, the year after my sabbatical, I reflected on the weeks in the jungle when I found my mind and my heart dwelling on the myriad ways I have caused harm and grief to myself and others. As I walked through the wilderness on my own I listed them in my head, and the weight of them was very great and the sadness as big as the forest.

I named as much as I could. I named the people if I knew or could remember their names, I named the places, I recalled the experience, the feelings; I allowed myself no quarter, I lost myself in a thicket of regret, pushing through the humid forest and owning the failures of my life.

As well as individual, personal sin there was my connivance in and engagement in structural sin: British society's complicity in the legacy of empire and the legacy of slavery, my role as a middle-class white man with colonial ancestors. The casual destruction of the resources of the world. There I was, in one of the last refuges of wilderness on earth, reflecting on the way we are devouring nature as if it was a pre-dinner snack.

I let it all go. You are forgiven, I told myself. In the traditional words of the absolution at the end of confession:

> Our Lord Jesus Christ, who hath left power to his Church to absolve all sinners who truly repent and believe in him, of his great mercy forgive thee thine offences: And by his authority committed to me, I absolve thee from all thy sins, In the Name of the Father, and of the Son, and of the Holy Ghost. Amen.[24]

Or, in the words of Jesus, 'Go ... and do not sin again' (John 8.11).

Did it help? Yes. It lifted me. I have laboured under the weight of my failures for most of my life. I have apologized and apologized but never believed myself to be adequate, in spite of 20 years of assuring others that they are infinitely loved. I have never trusted my own forgiveness, and perhaps that locked me into the spiral of destruction and despair. In *metanoia* – repentance, a new mind – we are being invited to discover love, perhaps for the first time.

I still give myself over to anger and envy and desire; but I can, usually, break the cycle. If I were to identify a moment of transformation, it would be that day in the dark of the jungle, when the weight of my sin was the gloom of the shadows of the trees around me, but the lightness was brighter than the sun breaking through in momentary clearings. I discovered and continue to rediscover a trust in the reality of love and the meaningfulness of repentance. I believe in the hope of resurrection.

2010

A Sunday morning in September. The 9 o'clock service is quiet, usually, and we rarely get visitors. That day there were two. Afterwards I greeted them. One was from Nigeria, Ade, newly arrived to study for a master's at King's. The other introduced himself.

'My name is Shanon. I'm from Malaysia, I'm gay, and I'm Muslim. I'm looking for an inclusive place of worship.'

'Welcome!' I said. 'You'd better come to tea.'

He had a friendly and warm face. He was in his early thirties, I judged, and perhaps a little nervous – but not afraid, it seemed, to be himself. Or perhaps he was being pre-emptively cautious. He came to tea, and asked lots of questions about the church, about me, about London, and I asked him lots of questions, about Malaysia, about his life. I discovered he had been a (now repentant) oil company executive, a musician, a playwright, an activist, a journalist. I held forth, a bit too much. He listened well. He came to tea again the following week. He came to church again on Sunday. He was planning to be here for a year, on a Chevening scholarship, sponsored by the Foreign Office. Thank you, Your Majesty!

The glint of phosphorous in slate-dark waves. Out of the darkness, hope.

17

Rubber hits the road

1989

Historically, the church has been for many a safe place where remaining unmarried raised fewer eyebrows. 'Beware the Anglo-Catholics,' wrote Evelyn Waugh, 'they're all sodomites with unpleasant accents.' Expectations of marriage and children were often sidestepped by priests who showed exceptional devotion in inner-city parishes, which, without those people, might have struggled to survive.

But that situation began to change in the 1970s, when open conflict over questions of sexuality started to erupt. The conflict has formed a backdrop to my life since I found my way back into the Church of England. It started, for me, before I was ordained. As the Director of Southwark Diocesan Housing Association I attended a chilly clergy conference in a holiday camp on the north Norfolk coast in 1989, off season, wind whipping sand off the tops of the dunes. Jack Spong, the progressive liberal bishop from the United States, was invited to speak, following the publication of his controversial but beautiful book *Living in Sin? A Bishop Rethinks Human Sexuality*. He had been vilified in the United States as he led the charge towards full inclusion of lesbian and gay people in the Episcopal Church.

The nastiness of the opposition. The conference organizers had the bright idea of putting up a graffiti board for any comments or contributions during the conference. Anonymous traditionalists plastered it with slogans. 'Leviticus 18.22: If a man lie with a man as with a woman it is an abomination. Spong is the child of the devil. Sodomites are damned.'

The bishop spoke with passion and wisdom about the abuse

of scripture, and made me weep. After he had spoken, a small group of us gathered in a cold seminar room and founded the Southwark Diocesan Lesbian and Gay Support Network – SLAGS, as it became known. We built the network by going through the Diocesan Directory and contacting the people we knew, or suspected, were lesbian or gay. The meeting dates and locations were kept secret. Our gatherings offered times of solidarity and support as we heard story after story of discrimination and rejection. A meeting attended confidentially by the then Bishop of Southwark became stuck in a repeating loop: he asked not to be told about any relationships, because if he officially knew he would be required to take action. I felt for him as he tried to negotiate the church's inability to acknowledge clergy partnerships.

Fifteen years later, the scandal of Jeffrey John's resignation from his post as Bishop of Reading was front page news for months. Out of it came Inclusive Church, initially a petition started by Giles Fraser to the General Synod seeking parity of treatment for LGBTQ+ people, black people and women. The petition was signed by thousands of people within days and launched at a Eucharist at St Mary's, Putney, attended by 450 people. After not many months it became clear that there was a need for an organization that brought together all these issues, alongside the various specific groups in the church – including the Lesbian and Gay Christian Movement, Changing Attitude, Women and the Church, and the Association of Black Clergy. I became Secretary and, later, Chair, and led Inclusive Church until 2011.

The conflict has been venomous. It has touched every corner of life in the church. Attitudes towards same-sex relationships have become a lightning rod, a signifier for orthodox Christian belief. An unholy triangle of agitation – the USA, sub-Saharan Africa, England – has threatened and huffed, supported by conservatives in Canada and Sydney, Australia. Many bishops stayed away from the Lambeth Conference in 2008, trying to undermine the legitimacy of the historic Anglican Communion.

Inclusive Church liaised closely with bishops and policy people in Church House and Lambeth Palace. I tried to have conversations with those who took a different view but they ran rapidly into the mud. I saw the strain being placed on Rowan Williams and was not surprised he took the escape route offered by Magdalen College. But his going did little to turn down the heat.

In 2009 the controversy over LGBTQ+ inclusion in the Church of England was virulent. Civil partnerships had been in place since 2003, and there was talk of equal marriage. What was the church's response? To oppose, oppose and oppose again. The Archbishop stood up in the House of Lords and opposed, and his fellow bishops opposed too. The Bishop of Salisbury wrote a letter in favour of same-sex marriage and was thoroughly and quickly squashed. People came and asked me to bless their relationships. I sent them away, saying that we were not permitted to do such a thing. My heart ached as I said it, but them's the rules and I could do nothing about it. This institution that is meant to be about love is responsible for such pain. How could I represent it? And what was it doing to my soul to be holding the ring in this way?

2013

Out of the blue, the rules turned round to bite me. I had spent much of my life negotiating homophobia, internalizing it sometimes to the point of dysfunction, or trying to shrug and laugh it off. There came a time when these careful negotiations began to fall apart, and the life I had constructed with Shanon felt suddenly as fragile as a soap bubble.

The phone call seemed innocuous. A courtesy call – nothing to worry about. Jo, the Archbishop of Canterbury's chaplain: she suggested a coffee, a visit to the parish, she would like to see what I'm up to, how the congregation is doing. Fine, do come, I said, and we fixed a date a few weeks ahead.

This parish was created out of the parish of St Mary, next to Lambeth Palace, in the early nineteenth century. So the Archbishop of Canterbury is patron of St John's. It is a significant role – patrons are responsible for appointing the vicar – but once the appointment is made, the patron usually has little more involvement. I was pleased that Jo wanted to come, and that Lambeth Palace was showing an interest in the parish.

We met on the steps at the front of church. She was wearing Doc Marten boots, which gave me a kindred affection. For many years I wore DMs, blue, nine hole. They replaced a black pair with red laces. I still have them, buried in the shoe cupboard.

We had a perfectly fine tour of the church. I had done the tour many times. We started in the church and discussed how much like a barn it felt, and then we went down to the crypt, into the vaulted, smelly damp part, and I took my visitor into the boiler room, which was dark and decrepit and felt like the engine room of an old tramp steamer, past the Mendelssohn Room, and up the dingy fire escape at the north-east corner of the church, into the openness and beauty of the churchyard. Back to the vicarage, kettle on, biscuits out, chat.

This parish is unusual in having two patrons: the Archbishop of Canterbury and the Church Pastoral Aid Society (CPAS). A quirk of history brought them together. In the nineteenth century – around 1860 – there was a row. The newly emergent evangelical movement – low church, Protestant, opposed to such dangerous Romish traditions as candles on altars – fell out with the vicar of St John's and managed to get permission to carve out a smaller parish a few streets away. St Andrew's was very different, liturgically and theologically – it eschewed high-church practices such as a weekly Eucharist. CPAS's predecessor saw its mission as establishing a truly scriptural Christianity, resisting Romish liturgy.

The two churches lived uncomfortably alongside each other for 80 years. Then both were bombed. St Andrew's was rebuilt on another site, in Short Street, opposite where the Young Vic theatre stands now. A big 1950s brick thing. It felt like the inside of an empty barge. The congregation shrunk, and shrunk, and in the end it was, with some difficulty, merged with St John's.

So I had two patrons: one the leader of the Church of England and the Anglican Communion and the other a prominent institution in the evangelical firmament. Which skewered me, very neatly, on the horns of the Church of England's current dilemmas over sexuality.

The problem was this: when I was appointed to St John's I was single, and so, technically, could be considered celibate. CPAS were prepared to agree to my appointment on that basis.

Because of a legal technicality (I was appointed as priest-in-charge, and after five years the appointment must, by law, be converted to vicar, unless there are strong reasons why not), both the Archbishop and CPAS now had to reaffirm my appointment. But it was common knowledge that I had begun a relationship, and was therefore no longer single. CPAS were therefore unwilling to confirm me in post.

Jo explained all that, in a conversation that felt both awkward and surprising. As the meeting continued I felt more and more uneasy.

'So, what are the next steps?' I asked. 'What does the Bishop of Southwark say?'

'We're all consulting at the moment, and we'll need to consult more. I hope to come back to you soon.' She stood up. 'I'm sorry,' she said. 'It's a difficult situation.'

'You're telling me,' I muttered as she vanished back into the churchyard. Shanon was out, teaching at King's. He came home at lunchtime and I recounted the conversation to him. I had not really taken it in at that stage, but as I told him his face grew more and more drawn.

'I don't understand. What does it mean? Why do they have to confirm you in post?'

I explained again. We were standing in the living room and his face was in shadow.

'So it's my fault?'

'No, my love, it's not your fault. It's not anyone's fault – except, perhaps, the C of E's as we're in this absurd position where lesbian and gay clergy are meant to be celibate.'

'Can I just say, for the record, that I'm glad you're not?'

'What, even if it gets me sacked and we're turfed out of here?'

'It will have been worth it.'

I laughed. 'We can sleep under the arches and come to the vicarage for sandwiches.' Shanon didn't laugh back.

'You're serious, aren't you. Could this really mean we have nowhere to live and you have no job?'

'At the moment it looks like that. But I'll need to take advice.'

'You better had! Come here.' He opened his arms and gave me a hug, but when we separated I hardly felt better.

'We'd find something,' I said. 'But let's hope, and pray, we don't have to.'

Shanon and I waited in the vicarage for more information. We spent long hours turning the conversation over, looking at it from different angles as one might look at a lump of coal. I had a deep sense of unease as I began to realize on how narrow a tightrope I was walking. That was part of the problem. My public self and my private self, managed with such care until now, were about to collide. Had I been single the pretence could have been maintained. The fact of our relationship meant that a blind eye could no longer be turned. CPAS was not willing to be seen to be condoning what they identified as unbiblical, regardless of the human cost involved.

We were experiencing the vulnerability that is the consequence of prejudice. We felt powerless; our fate was to be decided by people who may not have the best interests of us or the parish at heart. The rock upon which I thought I had built my house was turning out to be as soft as pumice, friable and easily eroded.

We awaited further instructions from Lambeth Palace. We had agreed it would be better not to involve the congregation; no need to create unnecessary anxiety. It was hard to believe that all that I was building and trying to create could be brought to an abrupt halt, but I had heard too many sad stories of decisions within the church, based directly or indirectly on homophobia, to be confident about the future.

'This is like Malaysia,' said Shanon. 'Like the religious police there. I didn't expect this in England!'

'I feel like an insect held in the palm of a CPAS hand,' I said. 'These conservative organizations. They've nailed their colours to seven Bible verses. It's become an article of doctrine for them, a badge of orthodoxy. There can be no compromise.'

'But the Archbishop's not like that!'

'This isn't the Archbishop. They both have to agree. It's

CPAS. When I was appointed I was single. So, actually, yes, on reflection, it *is* all your fault.'

'Oh, right, great, thanks so much! That's just what I need, right now.'

'Well, if we *were* celibate it wouldn't be an issue,' said I.

'So if that's what it takes – let's be celibate. Tell them we're devoted but our friendship is pure. I sleep in the spare room and the closest we ever get to each other is to shake hands at the Peace in church. Tell them we're crazy about each other but our faith is more important to us than mere physicality.' He was laughing but underneath he was serious.

'It's worth a try,' said I. So I made a phone call. A few days later I had a reply. Thanks for the suggestion – we're horrified you had to suggest it – let's not complicate things any more than they are at the moment.

The weeks ticked past. The date the Archdeacon and I had tentatively fixed for the induction service neared, and I had no idea if it would happen or if in three months' time I would be out of a job and we would be homeless. I scoured the internet to try to discover the legal position. No guarantees were available for priests-in-charge. They hold their posts on licence for as long as the goodwill of the bishop lasts. Could I really be evicted and made jobless without so much as an appeal hearing? It seems I could.

I decided to take the mountain to Muhammad. I knew the chief executive of CPAS quite well, for we had had conversations in the past – suppers in London where we tried to build friendships before broaching the issues that divided us. The suppers went quite well. We spent much of the time discussing the chickens that one of our number kept in her garden. When the rubber hit the road we could find little common ground, but a relationship had been built, and so I organized a lunch with John in an Italian restaurant on the Cut.

I walked there feeling anxious but clear about the approach I would have to take. John had already taken his seat when I arrived. We greeted one another and ordered – bolognese for him and puttanesca for me. Lunch was friendly. We talked about shared interests, people we knew, General Synod – and about the issue at hand. The conversation felt surreal. John acknowledged how well the parish seemed to be doing, and how encouraging he found the reports he'd had. But the fact remained that it was well known that I was in a relationship, and CPAS could not be seen to be condoning such a thing, and therefore they were in a difficult position. Not half as difficult as mine, I thought, but held my tongue.

We talked around the subject, but he seemed determined. Until in the end I thought it was time to try to bring the matter to a head. I took a glug of wine and said, 'Perhaps I can make this easier. As far as I read it, I can continue in this role until or unless the bishop withdraws my licence. So, regardless of what you do or don't do, I can remain in this post as priest-in-charge until I retire, unless the Bishop of Southwark decides to take away my licence, which I am very confident he wouldn't. I'm pretty sure that a decision by CPAS to withhold its agreement to my appointment as vicar would simply mean that I would continue as priest-in-charge. So, either way, you can't be rid of me.'

He looked a little pale.

'I suppose that, from where we are,' he said, 'it wouldn't be right for us to withdraw an approval that we have already given. If we hadn't agreed to your appointment in the first place, then we wouldn't be having this conversation. But it does put me in a difficult position – particularly if you are planning to campaign publicly against the CPAS position and in favour of same-sex marriage.'

I was not expecting that.

'John, I've been having these conversations for 25 years. To be honest with you, it's beginning to feel long enough. My focus is moving on to climate change. That feels even more urgent. But I can't stop being myself!'

We parted and still I had no answer. Shanon and I were still in limbo.

18

Prayers in a church?

2014

What I have seen is this: to truly understand these moments of transcendence it takes a community. A group of motley people in all their rumbustious queerness, all their reckless diversity.

A million bats fly out of the Mulu Caves in Borneo as the tropical night draws in and they prepare to travel to their feeding groups many miles away. They fly in great circles, a doughnut of a hundred thousand bats flying in a ring. Why? Because then the bat hawks that are waiting for their evening meal are less able to catch their prey. The bats know that if they fly in circles together they are less easy targets, more likely to live to swallow another thousand mosquitoes.

If a community is to flourish it must be based on mutual love and mutual care. The transactions must be gift transactions, not commerce. The complex set of relationships between micro-rhyzoidal fungus and the trees alongside in which they live is a relationship of gift. The fungi and the roots swap sugar and starch and oxygen, and in so doing they discover a sort of flourishing that alone would never be possible. Robin Kimmeridge Hall's book *Braiding Sweetgrass* speaks of the relationship between sweetgrass and the indigenous tribes who braid it, collectively, into rope strong enough to build a bridge across an abyss.

Love is a gift. It can only be offered freely, never extracted. Love is the earthly manifestation of the infinite life force that is named by religious traditions as God.

Behind love lies justice. For unless we are equal the gift is at risk of being improperly given and received. A gift to the powerful can too easily become a tribute, a payment extracted by the strong from the weak. In a society where all are held in equal respect, where black lives really do matter and the world of LGBTQ+ people is not shadowy and marginal but open-hearted and integrated, the process of giving and receiving can be a manifestation of love. Love and justice are inseparable companions.

How to live out that vision. That's the challenge I face, at St John's and in my daily life.

An email arrived from Bishop Malkhaz Songulashvili, the Metropolitan Bishop of the Evangelical Baptist Church of the Republic of Georgia. He had contacted me, by recommendation. He suggested meeting. My acquaintance with bishops from Georgia is slight, and so we arranged to have coffee in Waterloo Station. He was a big man with a big beard, just as a it should be – but he was Baptist, not Orthodox, and it sounded from what he said as though he ploughed a lonely furrow in his home country.

'My friend,' he said, over coffee in Costa, 'I have a task for you. I hope that you will accept it.'

'Try me.'

'I have been in Oxford, studying, but now I have to return to Tblisi. I do what I can there, to make the gospel of love known to all people. It is difficult, you'll understand, the people are harsh.' He looked at me, a gaze full of compassion. 'You know these things, you and your group.'

'Which group?'

'Inclusive Church. I know about your work, trying to make the Church of England more inclusive – that's why I wanted to see you.'

This felt weird. Sitting in a coffee shop in Waterloo Station with a Georgian bishop, who I thought might be about to come out to me … what was the task I was about to be offered?

'We're not having quite the success I was hoping for,' I said. 'We know more about the lack of inclusion than we do about making a difference.'

'Well, we're all locked in similar struggles,' said Bishop Malkuz. 'That's why I need your help. I have friends, in Oxford, whom I have been supporting. I am anxious, for they struggle, and I want to be sure that they have people looking out for them. They are a small group of wonderful young Muslims. They have taken the name Inclusive Mosque, and they want to create a place where Muslims can pray and share their lives in safety, regardless of who they are. Will you help?'

'Of course, Bishop. Of course I will. Is it coincidence, that they are called Inclusive Mosque?'

'Not at all. They modelled it on your group – Inclusive Church. That's why I came to you!'

Before long I met them and warmed to them at once. They had a vision for a mosque in London which was truly inclusive, where Sunni could pray next to Shia, where women and men could lead prayers equally, where people could explore the Qur'an and the Sunnah with like-minded people and people who would challenge them. They were idealists in a world where even to call yourself a Muslim is to open yourself up to potential abuse. They were – are – a delightful group of men and women, some strictly observant, some in hijab, some converts, some gay or lesbian or trans.

I received an invitation to supper at Taz, a Turkish restaurant near London Bridge. Twenty of us gathered around the table to eat dolmades steeped in vinegar and cool tzatziki. Conversation sparkled, fresh as a stream, northern accents from Pakistani Brits.

'We have a strong speaker for International Women's Day,' said Aisha. 'Dr Amina Wadud. You'd love her, Giles: she speaks powerfully.'

'But there's a problem,' said Iram. 'We have nowhere to hold the prayers.'

'Can't you borrow a mosque?' I asked, stupidly. 'Don't they have rooms you can use?'

'If they did, we wouldn't need Inclusive Mosque,' said Aisha. 'They won't permit a woman to lead prayers, and they'd never accept an out LGBTQ+ speaker.'

Without a second thought, I said, 'Come to us!'

'Are you sure?' said Iram. 'Don't you have to get permission or something?'

'Why should I need to do that?' I said. 'We're an inclusive

church, aren't we, and you want to pray. What could be the problem?'

St Andrew's, our smaller church, was booked for the day they needed. So I reserved St John's on the church online calendar. I entered *Inclusive Mosque, Friday Prayers*, and Lorraine sent them a booking form (free-of-charge booking, of course).

Fridays are my day off so I usually avoid the building. But I decided, at about 12.30, to pop over and see how it was all going. I found a hubbub. The chairs had been moved to one side, and prayer mats had been laid across the floor, with the leaders' mat facing towards the south-east corner of the church, towards Mecca. At that time, the life-sized statue of a naked blue Jesus was still on that side of the church, too. Naira saw me and came across. She wore a green shalwar kameez and an anxious frown.

'Giles, this place is perfect. Thank you!' She hugged me quickly. 'But, I wonder, is it OK if we move Jesus?' She pointed towards him. 'It's just that – his genitals – they're at eyeline if we're kneeling …'

So I slipped him out of the way and turned him round. Amina arrived, swathed in a sky-grey hijab, eyes light, a look of warmth. Before long it was time to start.

'Salaam aleikum!' called Naira. 'Salaam aleikum! Greetings, everyone!'

'W'a'leikum salaam!'

'You are all very welcome! Whether you are Muslim or Christian or Jew or none of the above, come and join us. Find your place on the mat.'

Around 100 people approached and, taking off their shoes, filled the prayer mats. I went forward. By then I'd been to prayers many times with IMI, and during Ramadan Shanon and I unrolled our prayer mats and prayed at home. William Dalrymple, in *On the Holy Mountain*, writes that early Christian prayers were physical in the same way, derived in turn from ancient Jewish prayers. Bowing before God, symbolic humility, relinquishing uprightness for the sake of the soul. Shanon laughs when I comment that they are 'very aerobic'. The ritual, the formalism: it reminds me of Morning Prayer.

I joined the back row, staying on the edge because I was look-ing after the sound system. The prayers started – someone was videoing the service – Muslims, Christians, Jews and Hindus praying together. Some stood at the back, watching and joining in their own way. Some of the women had their heads covered, scarlet and gold scarves glittering in the sunlight.

When I pray with Muslims I repeat the Lord's Prayer and the Gloria, or the Hail Mary, under my breath, as I don't under-stand the Arabic. We bowed, and prostrated, and stood, and bowed, and prostrated, and stood, and after the prayers we sat and listened to the khutbah – the address. Amina spoke of the image of God that we hold in our hearts, opening up the concept of God, pushing us gently beyond anthropomorphic and gendered theistic straightjackets. There was nothing she said that I could not have said in a sermon. After the prayers, thinking it would be good to use the scripture shared by Jew, Muslim and Christian, I read from Psalm 139, one of the most universal of psalms:

> If I take the wings of the morning,
>   and settle at the furthest limits of the sea,
> even there your hand shall lead me,
>   and your right hand shall hold me fast. (Ps. 139.9–10)

I gave thanks, to God, to Allah, the God whom we share. Amen, said everyone – or ameen, the Arabic pronunciation.

There was lunch – falafels and houmous, vegan halal and kosher – and there was conviviality and delight, and everyone had a lovely time and helped put the chairs back and ready the church for Sunday worship.

The following day a video of the service was put online. I was delighted by how well the event had gone, and how glad the people of IMI were to have a place in which they could know that they were welcome. I joyfully tweeted about it and thought no more of it. The tsunami came later.

19

The heat rises

2017

A misty holiday on the south coast, in Dorset. We stayed in a
farm cottage at the end of an unmade track. Across the field
near an ancient hedge stood a mediaeval church, ruined now,
the roof open to the sky, a niche empty of its statute next to
where the altar must have been. A shrine, according to the faded
notice, to the local saint, St Bradogand or some such. The building constructed of grey stone among tenuous peasant dwellings
of wattle and daub long since vanished. This ruined shrine is all
that remains of the smallholders who eked out a living on this
storm-tossed hillside. I thought of Mother Julian, of the persist-
ence of prayer, of those ancient buildings still standing when all
vestiges of the lives around them had vanished.

> As he was setting out on a journey, a man ran up and knelt
> before him, and asked him, 'Good Teacher, what must I do
> to inherit eternal life?' Jesus said to him, 'Why do you call me
> good? No one is good but God alone. You know the com-
> mandments: "You shall not murder; You shall not commit
> adultery; You shall not steal; You shall not bear false witness;
> You shall not defraud; Honour your father and mother."' He
> said to him, 'Teacher, I have kept all these since my youth.'
> Jesus, looking at him, loved him and said, 'You lack one
> thing; go, sell what you own, and give the money to the poor,
> and you will have treasure in heaven; then come, follow me.'
> When he heard this, he was shocked and went away grieving,
> for he had many possessions. (Mark 10.17–22)

I love that story, especially these words: 'Jesus, looking at him,
loved him'. Jesus understood what was clutching at the feet of

the young man, and told him, but he was unable to respond and went away grieving.

I wrote earlier about the key words in Christian theology: *agape* and *metanoia* – love and repentance. But as well as *agape* are other words for love, especially *eros*. For many centuries theology has mistrusted *eros*. It represents, according to the early Fathers, the dangerous side of love, the slippery path towards concupiscence. *Eros*, I was solemnly told as a teenager, was to be avoided. *Agape* was the right kind of love, *eros* the wrong kind.

How sad that is. It takes its cue from the coolness of some Greek philosophers. Aristotle, in the *Nichomachean Ethics*, writes of the ideal love as unpassionate friendship. Origen is said to have castrated himself to become like a eunuch for the love of God. Augustine, the author and begetter of so much guilt, writes in the *Confessions* at length about the wickedness of his life before converting – although he seems to me to protest too much, the wickedness extended only to his having a relationship with a woman to whom he was not married, and whom he put away as soon as he converted to Christianity.

Eros, desire, should be at the heart of theology. Jesus, looking at the man, loved him. The best of love seeks, passionately, the best for the beloved. Sarah Coakley's influential work on the Trinity, *God, Sexuality and the Sacred*, makes a powerful case for reclaiming a theme that has been subterranean since the earliest years of the church, the theme of God's passionate desire for humanity, which draws us in and calls us to be our authentic selves.

Eros is what draws us more deeply into the forest. The Song of Solomon names it:

> Set me as a seal upon your heart,
>   as a seal upon your arm;
> for love is strong as death,
>   passion fierce as the grave. (Song of Sol. 8.6)

The letters of Paul, read so often through a lens of fear, are transformed if fear is replaced by desire:

For I am convinced that neither death, nor life, nor angels, nor rulers, nor things present, nor things to come, nor powers, nor height, nor depth, nor anything else in all creation, will be able to separate us from the love of God in Christ Jesus our Lord. (Rom. 8.38–39)

The church has lost much by selling the reality of love short. One of the saddest questions in scripture is in the book of Genesis:

They heard the sound of the LORD God walking in the garden at the time of the evening breeze, and the man and his wife hid themselves from the presence of the LORD God among the trees of the garden. But the LORD God called to the man, and said to him, 'Where are you?' (Gen. 3.8–9)

I remember a morning walking home alone from a nightclub, through the brutalist Brandon Estate with its Henry Moore sculpture in the middle, at 5 or 6 o'clock in the morning, the dawn shining pink on the silvered clouds. I remember a feeling, the dawn rising. Meeting a boy, having a conversation, not going up to his flat, moving on, warmed by the mysterious light around me.

To understand the cosmos as bonded by love, the life force, is to understand that we are all bonded in relationship. It opens up a theology in which we humans can celebrate our dependence on the rest of creation instead of trying to dominate it. Above all it means that we can allow ourselves to trust. Trusting in the truth of love's desire for love (God *cannot* not love, for God is love) sets us free from the weeds that clutch. This is the radical truth that Francis, John of the Cross, Julian, Rumi, so many, understood so clearly. Yet still we struggle to celebrate love in our churches.

2014

Shanon and I waited for a response from Lambeth Palace. The date for the induction drew nearer and nearer and still there was no answer. I spoke to the Bishop and the Archdeacon, but they were none the wiser. We could do nothing but wait. Until, at last, word came from the Palace.

The word was good. Yes. We could go ahead. There was no indication as to what had changed ... simply, advice that the service could proceed and I could be, formally, declared the incumbent. On one level, that meant that nothing would change; on another, much changed, because I had greater security – as did Shanon – and the Church of England had, eventually, affirmed me in post.

The service we held was a service of celebration, although few in the parish knew of what had been going on behind the scenes – we had reached the view it was better not to report every twist and turn of the saga, not least because we did not want our relationship to be the focus of chat and speculation. But the moment when I was handed a legal document giving me the care of the souls of the parish was a moment of joy. The hairs stood up on the back of my arms. I caught Shanon's eye across the congregation. Phew. But, counteracting the phew, a real awareness of how fragile our position was, because of the endemic fear of human sexuality that has beset the church since its earliest years.

That same year – 2014 – the Marriage (Same-Sex Couples) Act was signed into law. Same-sex marriage had come much sooner than anyone (including me) in the Church of England had expected. The House of Bishops fought a rearguard action against the legislation. The Archbishop has reported the conversations he had in the robing room: what on earth did the Church of England think it was doing?

Once the legislation had passed, we were told that the House of Bishops would produce a response to the new legislative situation. We waited with little expectation but some hope for something that might open up a path towards inclusion.

True to form, eventually a report was produced: *Marriage*

and Same Sex Relationships after the Shared Conversations.[25]
The report felt like a slap in the face followed by a sop or two.
Clergy were encouraged to use 'maximum freedom' under
the current rules when offering pastoral support to LGBTQ+
couples. There was to be a teaching document from the House
of Bishops to help the church think through where we are now.
Other than that, nothing.

The report was to be presented to the General Synod so that
we might 'take note' of its existence. I had been elected chair
of the General Synod Human Sexuality Group the year before.
Emails began to circulate. A meeting was convened. Unexpected
people emerged as supporters. Deans of cathedrals, evangelical
archdeacons, people with weight in the hierarchy. Members of
the House of Bishops remained publicly united but we knew
that there was unrest behind the closed doors.

We were angry, and the anger became focused on some case
studies that were offered for discussion, to be followed by a
debate. The worked examples felt patronizing and as though
LGBTQ+ people were being essentialized, turned into issues
instead of being treated as people.

We called on other organizations on Synod – Women and the
Church, Affirming Catholicism, Accepting Evangelicals. When
Synod started, in the august and usually tranquil setting of
Church House, Westminster, we gathered in knots in corridors
and meeting rooms to develop a plan. Jayne took a lead on
publicity and media. We held a photo opportunity for out
LGBTQ+ members of Synod standing on the steps of Church
House. The idea emerged that we boycott the workshops. 'No
talking about us without us', went the cry, and because we had
been outside the room as the House had prepared its report we
would remain outside the room as they asked us to discuss it.
We gathered, instead, in a church nearby – St Matthew's, Westminster – and, we learnt, the Archbishop of Canterbury would
come to join us.

That Synod, in February 2017, three years after the Act had
been passed, began to feel as though it might be a watershed
moment. Now that the country had moved on, accepting equal
marriage almost without a murmur, the church's situation

seemed untenable. But Synod is a conservative body that tends, in the end, to vote with its bishops, and we had no idea whether we would be able to muster enough votes to reject the report.

The Archbishop came and spoke with us. We told stories of exclusion and compromise, hope and fear. He listened to us and answered our questions as best he could. He apologized, as I remember, and encouraged us to vote to take note but without, I think, much hope that we would change our minds.

The following day the grand debating chamber at the heart of Church House was completely full. The seats are small and we were squeezed in, collar to collar. There were anxious conversations beforehand in the tea room. Who will vote with us, and who with the bishops? The hubbub continued until the gavel was banged against the panelling. We rose for the entrance of Aiden, the Chair for this debate. He explained the rules; 150 people had put in to speak, so the speech limit was three minutes from the start. I had no idea if I was to be called but thought it likely I would be.

The Bishop of Norwich introduced the motion. He emphasized no change was proposed to canon law, and that he had been contacted by many people.

Speeches followed, one after another. The first speech was powerful – from the Archdeacon of Dudley:

> It is time for the silent middle to become vocal and to be clear that many of us who are still evangelicals, still seeking to be biblically orthodox, are now acknowledging our Scripture interpretation was flawed. We must ensure all voices are heard and all people are valued, welcomed and affirmed.

We warmly applauded the people we agreed with, and gave more tepid responses to the people who said they were going to take note. At last I heard my name called by the Chair. My heart turned over as I moved towards the lectern. I had scribbled all over my speech. I knew time was against me. Nerves. Fear. I must remember to say my name and my number. I must speak slowly and clearly. I must not get angry. Here goes.

I have heard a lot during the conversations running up to this debate about the need to take the middle ground with us. Well, I stand before you as a member of the middle ground. I am vicar of a middle-of-the-road parish, St John's, Waterloo. Our electoral roll has increased under my tenure from 80 to 127. We have five people thinking about ordination, of whom two are under 20. We have trebled our congregational giving and have doubled our parish share. It feels as though we must be doing something right and yet St John's is seen as a dangerous parish, one to be treated with kid gloves. Why? Because the vicar is gay and has a partner. So our story, which should be one of success and delight, is one of mistrust and fear.

I have a real problem with this notion of maximum freedom. I am afraid that what it makes me think of is saying to a prisoner in his cell, 'You have maximum freedom to walk around the cell but of course we can't open the door for you ...' I know that there is a huge amount of fear around, but the howls of anger and pain that greeted this report must be enough for us to say we can do better ... Please, let us try again. Let us use our wisdom, our knowledge and our faith and let us take time to produce something that confidently speaks to the gospel for the whole of England. Please vote not to take note.

I sat down and breathed out, relieved that the moment had passed. Speeches continue, until at last it was time to vote.

'Am I for or against?' I asked Jayne.

'Against, silly!'

I pressed the button on the voting machine and watched my vote go. We waited for the result, murmuring, anxious. Finally the Chair called for our attention so that he could announce the result.

This is a counted vote by Houses. Can I remind the Synod, especially those in the gallery, that it is the custom of the Synod to receive the result of votes in silence.

The voting was as follows. In the House of Bishops, those in favour 43, against 1, with no recorded abstentions; in the House of Clergy, 93 in favour, 100 against, with 2 abstentions; in the House of Laity, 106 in favour, 83 against, with 4 recorded abstentions. So the motion was lost.

Jayne and I clutched hands as silently the result was received. We had done it. The report had been rejected, and the Church of England would have to try again. What would happen now? The next day, a letter was published from the archbishops.

First, we want to be clear about some underlying principles. In these discussions no person is a problem, or an issue. People are made in the image of God. All of us, without exception, are loved and called in Christ. There are no 'problems', there are simply people called to redeemed humanity in Christ ... We need a radical new Christian inclusion in the Church. This must be founded in scripture, in reason, in tradition, in theology and the Christian faith as the Church of England has received it; it must be based on good, healthy, flourishing relationships, and in a proper twenty-first-century understanding of being human and of being sexual.

We wondered what a 'radical new Christian inclusion' might look like. But I was glad that something might happen. Perhaps, for the first time in the church's history, the voices of LGBTQ+ people might be properly heard.

20

The vision refreshed

2017

I was so dismayed by the Chancellor's judgement against our renovation plans that for 24 hours I kept it to myself. Eventually I told David, our project manager, and Belinda, our church-warden. And, God bless them, they found chinks of light that I had not seen. They saw that the Chancellor was minded to grant a faculty for the less controversial aspects of the scheme – the insertion of a lift, the creation of a new staircase. They saw that the points at issue were related to the demolition of the Lady Chapel and the vestry. They wondered if we just might be able to find a way forward. We called a meeting with Mr Parry and Mr Filmer-Sankey and our other consultants, and, piece by piece, we began to put together a strategy. We might be daunted, said David, but we aren't beaten.

A few months later, Eric and James brought drawings to us and unfurled them on the table. The plans were good and responded to our needs. I had asked for a better link between the church and the crypt, for more accessibility, for the opening up of the crypt for community uses, for an improved entrance. All this they had taken into account as they looked again at the scheme. They reimagined the partition that was planned for below the balcony, separating the nave from the foyer and creating a new space of welcome. They re-envisioned the stair-case, sweeping downwards from the foyer. So far, so very good.

But the church itself was hardly touched. Caution, perhaps, had raised her flag. The ensemble around the high altar, they suggested, should remain as originally constructed in 1951, with some slight modifications – improved decoration, better lighting.

'I like what you're proposing,' I said. 'The staircase is beautiful, and will create a dynamic link with the crypt. The entrance is uplifting – it's exciting!

Eric nodded.

'But none of the problems we're facing with the worship space are solved. I think we have to be courageous. We have to find a way to make the worship space better for worship – otherwise, what's the point of doing all this work?'

A couple of months later, Eric and James came back with new ideas. They conserved the parts that we had been instructed to conserve, but they were disguised by a series of elegant solutions. A delicate filigree screen around the vestry and the Lady Chapel, offsetting the boxiness of the portacabin spaces. Two beautiful, angular structures at the west end of the church, picking up the screens at the front. 'The whole creating a sense', said Eric, 'of a pair of arms that would cup the altar and the worship space.' Two light-filled sculptural spaces in between, which would double as storage for chairs and timpani. All contained by a new decorative scheme that would refer back to the 1824 original but transform it for the twenty-first century.

I felt that sense of time kaleidoscoping, the past, the present, the future overlaid, a palimpsest. These plans would, if we could get them through, celebrate the best of the nineteenth, the best of the twentieth and the best of the twenty-first centuries. Yesterday today and for ever, all in one breath, all in one place.

There was, of course, the question of funding. When we started, the cost was estimated at £2.5 million. And then it grew, and grew, as the scope of the project grew, until the total estimate reached £5.5 million. But the parish had nothing, financially, to speak of.

The generosity of congregation members, the Borough of Lambeth and some trusts and foundations enabled us to leave first base and pay the architects and other consultants who were doing so much work for us. The fees clocked up, and up, and up. The fundraising proceeded apace. I and the team became experts at completing application forms, to the Big Lottery, to the Borough, to the Mayor, to the City Bridge Trust and many others. All were focusing on the community projects we wanted to undertake. Support for young people. Projects for refugees. Housing and homelessness. Pathways to work. Some were successful, some were not. The day we passed £1 million we opened a bottle of something sparkling. When we passed £2 million we opened another.

But the time it all took was immense – and the longer it took the more at risk our existing funding became. The whole thing was a juggling act, trying to make progress without leaving anyone behind.

We presented the new plans to the diocese, to the Twentieth Century Society, Historic England and Lambeth Council. We were given a donation of £100,000 to match other gifts, which lifted our hearts and the figures. The vision emerged from the fog but we still had no idea if what we wanted to do would ever be permitted. We thought it *might* be allowed, as we were preserving some of the key parts of the 1951 scheme. But the forces of opposition were powerful, and the previous judgement had been clear, and who knew if we had made enough compromises for the cards to fall our way?

2017

A couple of months after the Synod vote not to take note, as I was sitting in the garden on a hot July day, my phone rang.

'Giles? William Nye here, from Church House. I'm ringing about the proposed teaching document. We are setting up a coordinating group to bring it into being, and the House of Bishops needs some people on it who can act as consultants, so that we can be sure we hear a wide range of voices. The Archbishops wonder if you might be willing to be one of the consultants.'

It took me only an instant to say yes. Having asked for further reflection, having been involved so closely in the decision not to take note, how could I refuse to be part of the next stage of the process? I wondered what I could bring to the table, and decided that all I could bring was myself and the voice I had. So I committed myself to three years of hard work, hard engagement and hard listening.

After a few months the name for the process was agreed: 'Living in Love and Faith'. It turned out I was the only out gay man to be a consultant to the coordinating group, alongside my friend Tina who was the only trans woman on the group. We met, times beyond number, in Church House, in Lambeth Palace and in meeting rooms near King's Cross. We thrashed out how and what the resource might look like. We tried to be scrupulously fair to all points of view although I often found the description of my personhood, of that part of my identity as a 'point of view', problematic. As the archbishops had said, there are no issues, only people. I was trying to be myself in a world where the myself I was offering felt at times to be barely acceptable.

After three years, a suite of resources – a book, videos, podcasts, a course – was published, under the title *Living in Love and Faith*.[26] It included stories of LGBTQ+ Christian lives, made into videos through inspired editing. The book included theology, history, biblical studies, sociology, reflection, prayer, and an invitation from the House of Bishops. It would, we hoped, break new ground in those tired, circular disputes that had entrapped the church for so many years.

The jury is still out on the outcomes. At the time of writing, small steps – a form of prayer and liturgy, the recognition of clergy in partnerships – have been agreed by General Synod, but the pushback against these small steps has been very great. Even after the many years of prayer, engagement, conversation, listening and learning, positions remain entrenched. But something changed, for me, through the process. For the first time in my life in the church I was able to be myself without remainder or apology. To say, 'This is me' to bishops, deans and bureaucrats. To say, 'I am a Christian, I am a member of the Church of England, I am gay, I am in love.'

Even the smallest steps in this journey have been fiercely resisted. But there is hope. The hope is founded upon the truth that each of us is fully loved, fully loveable and fully equal before God. This is the truth that lies at the heart of the story of Jesus, and it is the truth I have been trying to articulate in my years as a priest. It is the truth from which the Church cannot escape, and it is the truth that keeps bringing refreshment and renewal to structures that would otherwise become sclerotic.

The innovative aspect of the *Living in Love and Faith* process was that it tried to give a voice to those who had until then been heard only on sufferance. I remember very clearly the moments where our stories were told and listened to. For the first time in my life in the church I had a sense of being there not through a conditional acceptance but because I too am equally held in the light of love.

We have not reached the promised land. But the kingdom is being constructed moment by moment. The quest for life in all its fullness starts with the vulnerable and risky moments when we acknowledge that we are all standing, equal and broken, before the altar. My part in the process felt like a moment of authenticity, and for that I am glad.

21

Fear and fury

2015

I was taught during my training that one role of a priest is to keep alive the rumour of God. Although now I reach beyond the Christian tradition and draw from spiritual traditions around the world, I was brought up in an almost entirely white Christian world. School taught us the history of the Crusades told from a European point of view. I imbibed an othering of Islam which was exacerbated by the reporting of 9/11 and its aftermath.

But my training at seminary and theological reading changed that. Interfaith seminars spoke of the shared heritage of the Abrahamic faiths – Islam, Judaism and Christianity – all finding their origins in the same small part of the Middle East, all sharing the same traditional scriptures. The Qur'an often refers to the characters and events of the Hebrew Bible – Moses, Elijah, the great flood, the destruction of Sodom. Mary is the only woman named in the Qur'an – a chapter is named after her – and Jesus is respected as one of the great prophets. Jesus, of course, was a Jew – something often forgotten in the waves of anti-Semitism that have racked the Christian world for over a millennium. I also learnt of the debt that Christianity owes to Muslim scholars from the years before the thirteenth century, who painstakingly preserved the writings of Greek philosophers, paying Nestorian Christians to translate them into Arabic, studying them in Spain and Sicily and the empires of the East until they were translated back into Latin by mediaeval monks and doctors, transforming the theology of giants such as Thomas Aquinas.

So it was an obvious thing to offer St John's to Inclusive Mosque. It was less obvious that I should receive a phone call from the *Daily Telegraph*'s religious affairs correspondent a couple of days later.

'Giles, can you tell me about the Muslim prayers you had at St John's?'

'It was a very moving event. We were glad to host it. It was a simple service of prayer, and a sermon, and refreshments. There were about a hundred people, mainly Muslim – and other faiths represented too.'

'I've seen it online. I heard you cleared the church?'

'No, we just moved the chairs so that they could put their prayer mats down. They were praying towards Mecca, of course, not towards the altar. All that was left untouched.'

'Oh, OK. It doesn't sound as though there's much there.'

'No, really, it was just prayers. I can't see that it's at all news-worthy.'

'I agree. Not much of a story.'

A few days later another phone call:

'Giles? Simon here. How are you doing?'

'Archdeacon! I'm fine, thanks. Nothing much going on. And you?'

'I could be better. This service you hosted, the Muslim prayers, it's causing a bit of a headache. You know there have been complaints to the Bishop? And to Lambeth Palace?'

'Really? That seems a bit extreme.'

'It's not. It's quite understandable. You do know you're not permitted to allow services of other faith traditions in church, don't you?'

'But they were just here to pray. They had nowhere else to go. What on earth is wrong with that?'

'It was against the rules. It's causing a situation. We'll need to talk.'

My inbox pinged. An email from someone whose name I didn't recognize.

Dear Father Goddard,

I have seen the video of your Muslim prayer service. I am horrified by what you allowed to happen in your church.

Don't you know that Muhammed is the antichrist and Muslims worship Satan? I hope you're defrocked.

Anne Richardson

I looked at the email address: .sa. – South Africa. Another came in, this time from Pakistan.

I'm a Christian in Lahore. We are being persecuted all the time. How dare you allow Muslims to pray in your church? They are evil and what you have done should be punished.

For the next few days my phone was ringing constantly and emails came in from all over the world. Mostly furious, some supportive. The diocese's Director of Communications told me to say nothing and not to respond to requests for interview. There were articles in *The Times* and the *Telegraph*. News items on the BBC website showing clips from the video, of Muslims praying in a church.

The Bishop of Kingston phoned, and we met in the vestry of St Andrew's, a boxy room with little natural light. He's tall and quietly spoken. He had always been supportive of me, but perhaps that was about to change.

'Giles, what have you done?'

'I ain't done nuffink!' I wanted to say. But that would not have been wise. 'All I wanted was to offer a place to pray. I thought that was what churches were for!'

'Of course it is. But it's more complex than that. Once something is online, people jump to conclusions. The images are very clear, and people find them shocking. They don't know the back story – that you were originally going to have the prayers somewhere else. Imagine how a Christian in a country where they are persecuted by Muslims might feel if they saw it?'

We were meeting on the margins of a conference, and the hallway outside was busy and noisy. The room, though, was quiet.

'This feels much bigger than it was intended to be. I was simply offering a place for friends to come and pray, and trying to be generous with our spaces. Inclusive Mosque is trying to break the mould by welcoming men and women to pray alongside each other. And for women to lead prayers. So they can't go to mosques. I thought we could help.'

'I understand that,' said Richard. 'But the legal position is not helpful either. It's fine to have prayers from other traditions in our worship. But it's definitely not all right for an entire service from another tradition to be held. There have been complaints at all levels. Some are saying that the church should be exorcised. They're saying that Islam is idolatrous, and that holding a Muslim service at St John's means that it has effectively become a mosque.'

'But that's absurd.'

'It's also that you called God Allah – that doesn't help. Even though, of course, that's what Arabic Christians across the Middle East call God. The Bishop of Southwark is under pressure as well – so we do have a situation and we have to find a way forward.'

'So what should we do?'

'I think we need you to apologize, as a first step. We won't achieve closure unless something is done. It might even be this or a disciplinary hearing.'

An act of instinctive generosity was morphing into something far more frightening. I realized it had offered a perfect opportunity for those in the church who saw Christian inclusion as a threat. Inclusive Islam meets inclusive Christianity – that was a step too far for the objectors. Islam and Christianity align at a very profound level but in too many places in the world the two faiths are at war. The simplicity of anathema is safer than the complexity of love.

I remembered an incident a few years before, when we were looking at a new software system for our church. Mark, the Secretary of our Church Council, was encouraged to visit a church in Wimbledon to learn about their experience with the system. He set up the appointment, but shortly afterwards had an email from the administrator:

I have discussed this with my vicar, and he says that because of the theological differences between our churches it would not be appropriate for you to come and visit.

Mark was bemused.

'Giles, can you explain this email?'

'Not really. There are churches within the C of E that come from a very puritan tradition. They see churches like ours as a real threat – they think we are propagating wickedness – and have decided that it's better to draw apart than to associate with potential sinfulness.'

'But I just wanted to learn about the software!'

'You might have contaminated them.'

That church was one of the sources of complaints to the Bishop about the Inclusive Mosque service.

The storm continued. Headline news on the BBC. I met with the Church Council.

'Why were we not told?' some asked.

'Because I didn't see it as potentially troublesome,' I replied. 'I don't tell you about all the bookings we have. This one has been turned into something much bigger than it should have been.'

The council was supportive.

'If we are to welcome lesbian and gay people unapologetic-ally,' said Peter, who came from Uganda 20 years ago, 'if we are to welcome all people, well then, I do not see why we should apologize for hosting prayers for Muslims. No, I do not see why we should apologize for that.'

The *Church Times* published a supportive article. Other letters and emails began to arrive from all over the place, affirm-ing what we had done – from Christians: 'I am writing from Gloucester to congratulate you on your action in welcoming Muslims to prayer.' And also from Muslims. But the threat of a disciplinary hearing did not lift, and I felt vulnerable. I did not answer phone calls from unrecognized numbers and I gave no interviews to the press.

'The only way out of this is an apology,' said the Bishop. Backwards and forwards we went, on the wording. Finally something was agreed, which apologized for the hurt caused and gave a commitment that I would not do it again. It was duly published. More headlines followed: 'Vicar apologizes for Muslim prayer service'.

I hoped that the apology would bring an end to the episode. The story died away from the front pages, but it did not disappear. Later in the year it re-emerged, as a result of an ordination service that was to involve members of St John's Waterloo and the church in Wimbledon.

'Giles? Bishop Richard here. We have another problem. The Wimbledon parish is refusing to be part of the ordination service if St John's Waterloo is present.'

My heart sank.

'I thought we had dealt with all that!'

'So did I. But they say that you apologized for the consequences, but not for the deed. I would like you to meet with them. See if we can get some sort of understanding. Could you come to my office, next week, on Wednesday?'

I took the train to Raynes Park, to the corner office on a nondescript street near the station. My accuser arrived late without apology. He was wearing a jacket and tie, in his mid-forties, severe eyebrows, unsmiling.

'There have been insufficient consequences from your actions. At the very least, you should resign your canonry from the cathedral, and it is no longer appropriate for Diocesan Synod meetings to be held at St John's. We require a further, more complete apology.'

I explained, once again, the sequence of events leading up to Amina Wadud's service. He was not interested.

'For us, what matters is that you are seen to have been disciplined.'

'It feels as though you want to put me in the stocks and throw things at me. As though you are really wanting to publicly humiliate me,' I said. 'I have explained. I will issue a further apology. But your attitude feels a long way away from the Christianity I try to live out.'

At the heart of the episode was a collision of world views. Not the clash of civilizations put forward as a thesis in 1992

by Samuel Huntington, between competing cultures and iden-
tities. On the contrary. The ties that bind Islam, Christianity
and Judaism – which bind all the major religious faiths – are
far stronger than the differences that separate us. The Qur'an,
like the Bible, contains moments of transformative beauty, and
moments of fear and anger. The Qur'an speaks of respect for
those of all faiths – 'Truly, there is no compulsion in religion'
– and of the light divine.[27] The 99 names of God in the Islamic
tradition – the Beneficent, the Merciful, the Utterly Just, the
Most Gentle – are a way of trying to describe the indescribable.
Sura after sura speaks of mystery and depth.

Violence and religion are rarely far apart, but the unthinking
pairing of Islam with violence is a deep injustice. The fall of so
many cities to Islam so quickly after its founding was in large
part to do with the inadequacy of those cities' governments at
the time. Christianity has appalling violence on its charge sheet:
the acts of the Crusaders; the massacre in Jerusalem when the
streets ran knee deep in the blood of Muslim men, women
and children; the destructive exploitation of the Middle East
by French, British and American empires in recent centuries.
Relations between Christianity and Islam have a tragic history
of misunderstanding and fear, exacerbated by power struggles
over oil.

The ordination went ahead. I continue to have good friendships with Inclusive Mosque. And the publicity was in the end
good for St John's; we were known for a while as the church
where the Muslim prayers were held, generously inclusive. In
a tiny way I was glad to have the chance to build friendships,
but our intentionally welcoming act fell victim to the dangers
of social media, and became caught up in a wider geopolitical
world of fear and mistrust.

22

Third rock from the Sun

2019

On sabbatical a few years ago I travelled to Borneo, where Shanon and I went trekking through the rainforest. We drove 30 kilometres off the high road to a national park called the Maliau Basin. We set off, following Kenneth our guide, with leech socks and water bottles and our backpacks weighted down with cameras and rain gear. We trekked along a poorly marked path that meant clambering over rocks and hauling ourselves up, up and up until we reached the edge of the basin and could see the land falling away from us on every side between the great dark trunks of the great dark trees, ironwoods and dipterocarps and mahogany that stretched up straight as plumb lines 150 feet to the thick green canopy above our heads, blanketing the light, the overstory trapping the heat of the tropical sun in the moist decaying air of the jungle.

The sounds of the forest buffeted our ears: screeches, whistles, whispers, buzzes of cicadas, crickets, gibbon, tree frog, more cicadas, more crickets. The cackle of huge hornbills, whose shadows we could see high up flickering through the canopies. We were truly in another world. Kenneth guided us through it, his extraordinary awareness spotting stick insects at 50 paces, treading silently on soft ground made of decades of decaying leaves and roots, providing sustenance for this generation of trees, which would, in turn, fall and provide sustenance for the generation thereafter, unto the end of time. A forest untouched, we thought, for millennia, where human beings should tread softly and leave no trace.

We sweated and struggled through the jungle until we reached the place of the spirits, the Nepenthes Hut. We had been warned that, there especially, the ancient spirits of the forest walked at night. We slept in the hut, shared by the people who guided us and the people who carried our food, and after the foresters had extinguished their last cigarettes and turned in, and the civet cat had stopped scratching for chicken bones just outside the camp, the unearthly sounds of the forest invaded my dreams and I wondered if I was indeed going to be consumed by the angry spirit who still seeks revenge for her brutal slaughter by a jealous god.

But of course it was all a mirage. On the way up to the Maliau Basin we drove through kilometre after kilometre of palm-forest monoculture. Dominic our friend told us of the village clearances and the destruction of the livelihoods of the indigenous people. Kota Kinabalu where we started our journey was like a frontier town in the wild west – which, in a way, it was – a British colonial centre back in the nineteenth century and now an oil and lumber town. We followed trucks as big as cargo ships bearing dead trunks of majestic trees 10 or 20 feet across, felled in an instant and dragged out across the clear-cut forest mud.

All around us was the evidence of greed unsatiated, the jungle destroyed by an ever increasing demand for palm oil to satisfy our desire for more body lotions, more shampoo, more ready meals, more ice cream. Greed feeds on greed. Want trumps need, and all around us the consequences are clear. Destruction, devastation, extinction. The orangutans are passing out of our lives. Pygmy elephants and clouded lynxes, Rajah Brooke's birdwing butterflies and long-tailed macaques survive only in reserves. The forests are going and the world will be broken without them.

2011

I was a book waiting to be opened when Siobhan came to see me, about a year after I arrived. She was the daughter of Quakers, a member of Climate Rush – a forerunner to Extinction Rebellion. She was 19, a student at King's, not someone who was shy about coming forward. She had already doorstepped the minister responsible for climate change and challenged his government to stop subsidizing fossil fuels.

We sat in the living room, drinking peppermint tea. She placed a folder on the floor by her feet. We chatted lightly until she fixed me with a firm stare and said:

'Giles, why are we taking money from Shell?'

'What money?' said I, bemused.

'For the Waterloo Festival. The sponsorship money.'

'Oh, that money! Because I asked them for some support towards the Festival and they gave it to me? It was £1,000, wasn't it? The Festival costs a lot to put on and this seemed like a good way to get funding. Shell funds lots of arts projects.'

'I thought we were an inclusive church?' said Siobhan.

'We are – or at least, we try to be,' said I. 'What does that have to do with £1,000 from Shell?'

'Don't you see the connection?'

'I'm afraid I don't.'

'What about climate justice? Isn't that important?'

'Of course.'

'Well – climate change is far more destructive for the poor than for the rich. Shell takes oil out of the ground, often in poor countries, and sells it, contributing directly to global warming. They're responsible for serious injustice around the world – you must know about the execution of Ken Saro-Wiwa in Nigeria. And yet you're taking funding from them.'

'But it's not Shell who are burning the oil – it's you and me,' I said, 'and all of us as we drive our cars or heat our houses.'

'Yes, and we should *all* change our ways, urgently, because climate change is real and it's coming down the tracks at us. But without fossil fuel companies there wouldn't be any climate change, and I think that as a church we should make a stand. Look, I have a graph here,' and she picked up the folder. 'This line is the proportion of CO_2 in the atmosphere, this line is global temperatures, and this line is the estimate of likely deaths from famine, disease or disruption. See how the figures increase as more CO_2 is pumped into the air from the burning of fossil fuels. Do you want to contribute to all these deaths?'

In 2009, the Climate Change Act had already been passed. Al Gore's film, *An Inconvenient Truth*, was out and had begun to make an impact. It was something I was aware of but I had not begun to make the connections. I cared about poverty, I rode a bicycle when I could and had got rid of my car, but that was because I hardly used it, not because of climate risk. Siobhan's challenge brought me up short.

We did not return the money to Shell after that first Waterloo festival, but Siobhan planted a seed. I realized that St John's could not flourish as a community of people unless we also paid attention to the world around us. We needed to remember the collective sense of enchantment to acknowledge the symbiotic relationship between earth and spirit.

From the conversation with Siobhan much emerged. As soon as I had learnt of the science of climate change and realized how steep the graphs were and how much humans were changing the atmosphere, I understood how urgent it was that things must change. Working with Operation Noah, I put a motion through the General Synod in 2014 which led to much more action from the Church of England. In the run-up to the big climate change talks in Paris in 2015, we started an interfaith climate change body – Faith for the Climate – which has created strong partnerships between people of different faiths, passionate about nature and justice for those suffering because of the climate crisis.

I thought back to those evenings on Hesworth Common when the sun was beginning to set, the folds of the Downs in shadow and yellowhammers singing fit to bust. I mourned their passing and was determined to take action.

2019

There came a particular Holy Week when Extinction Rebellion came to St John's and the parish was touched by stardust. Wispy people emerged like a shoal of sticklebacks. They wanted to create a new world and a new vision. Sharing and dreaming. There was a concatenation: two worlds collided, the boundaries blurred, police, church, establishment, anarchy. Working for a different way, more consensual. This is a fresh expression of activism. I was caught up in it.

There was something magical about Extinction Rebellion (XR) that first time. The crypt became a beautiful place. The police intervened like stag beetles in a float of butterflies. A little magic happened in the crypt, artworks, music, later the Red Rebels, their stark white faces and blood-red robes, walking, walking, walking. Conversation light but intense. There was light and life around the place, which seemed to lift the veil to another world. This is what we are dreaming of. This is how we can make it happen.

An email had arrived first, perhaps mid February: 'Dear Giles. I'm working with Extinction Rebellion. They're planning a major action in Central London and are looking for places of safety where they can sleep and store stuff. Can you help?'

It took only an instant to decide. Of course we could. We had, then, an empty crypt, long, damp, chilly, vacant. They could have a key to the crypt door. I replied and Helen passed my details on to a young man called Tom, who came to visit. Tom was the harbinger of the new arrivals, like the spies Joshua sent into Canaan, incipient beard, softly spoken, polite, clad in elfin robes. That last bit is not true, but he might just as well have been. I showed him the damp bit of the crypt, the former air-raid shelter. It was smelly and unprepossessing. But his eyes lit up when he saw it, and when he realized that there would be a kitchen available, with unlimited hot water, and there would be toilets and, wonder of wonders, showers, he was on fire.

'It'll be just a few people,' he said. 'Fifteen or twenty – key leaders who may need to rest when they're coming off the bridge. We'll keep the place closely supervised.'

'There won't be any trouble, will there?'

'We hope not! We're planning some actions, sure. But they're all non-violent.'

A quick conversation with the churchwardens. 'Giles, go for it. This is exactly what we should be doing.'

Passiontide began before I thought again of XR. They had not impinged on me, other than asking us to receive a couple of deliveries. I was gearing up to take part in the Holy Week drama. The soil beneath the church mirrors the darkness of the tomb and awaits the resurrection burst of light.

Monday of Holy Week dawned clear and warm. A happy spring day when the few surviving sparrows were busy collecting scraps for their nests, and blackbirds were hard at work on building theirs. I looked out of the window and saw, quietly gathering, another flock, more mysterious, people in red cagoulles and blue anoraks, many carrying backpacks. And behind them a forest had appeared, vivid birch trees and beeches clustered in pots on the tarmac space behind the church where normally the drinkers lurk and homeless people find a fleeting place of safety.

Mingling among the crowd – there were over a hundred people there – I had a feeling of quiet intensity. I spoke to one or two, older than me, men with shoulder-length grey hair and the remnants of a full beard, women in woolly hats and with determined eyes.

'My name is Theresa, and I have never been on an action before,' said one, proudly. 'I've come up from Somerset. Lots of us have. We're here to make sure that London knows how much we care. And how urgent it is!'

'Surely London knows that already?'

'Not in the slightest! We know that government hasn't told the truth. About the urgency – about the cataclysm that's on its way – or about the world that my children might inherit.'

She turned away, talking to a friend, and I'm left with the imprint of her passion. Somebody told me about the trees.

'They came up from Devon last night, on a low loader. It's so good that we were able to leave them here! I don't know what we would have done, otherwise!'

Tom was there, marshalling the forces. He was young enough to be my son and I would have been proud to have a son like him. I met Fletcher, too, a kind and lightly hirsute folk fanatic, and Gemma, Rachel, Gwendolen, all wreathed in smiles and determination.

At 11.30 a.m. the churchyard emptied, and I watched as they walked steadily on to the bridge, bringing with them on trolleys and wheels the trees and the bushes. It was a day of sunshine.

THIRD ROCK FROM THE SUN

The clouds had lifted. The churchyard was suddenly quiet. There was peace: but not for long, because quickly the traffic backed up down the Waterloo Road, and then there were the wails of sirens, and it became clear that the bridge had been blocked.

I checked the *Guardian* website. Marble Arch, Oxford Circus and Hyde Park Corner had been blocked as well. There were early pictures: a pink boat in the middle of Oxford Circus, bemused shoppers, women chaining themselves to the boat, people sitting in a circle in the middle of the road at Marble Arch. I didn't really know anything about Extinction Rebellion except that they had come together to encourage action against climate change. To take non-violent direct action. Some people had put themselves in a category that was new to me: arrestables. People willing to be arrested for obstruction so that they were sent to court, there to make their case that the government needs to act harder, faster and much more urgently on climate change.

In the afternoon I went up on to Waterloo Bridge. It was unbelievable. The trees had been laid out along the centre of the bridge, creating a woodland of eerie quiet. There was a truck parked slantways across the north–south carriageway, one side open to the world as a makeshift stage. A band was performing protest songs. There was a canteen under a green awning where cooks stirred vats of vegan food. There was a Quiet Space surrounded by greenery wherein people were sitting quietly, meditating. There was a hubbub, a mutter of smiling people dressed in t-shirts and camping trousers, sitting on the kerb, leaning on the railings. There were flags fluttering marked with the XR logo, 'Earth Protectors', and someone had written 'Save Mother Earth' along the anti-terrorist barrier between the road and the pavement. I looked out for the people I had met in the morning. A young woman stuck an XR sticker on my clerical shirt and smiled in response to my thanks. There were police at either end of the protest, standing quietly, a little bemused. The atmosphere was carnival but tense.

Back at the church, the door to the crypt was open and chairs were ranged around the forecourt. Amos was there, and Fletcher, and Daisy, smoking a roll-up.

'Hello, Father! Thank you *so much* for letting us use your space.'

'That's OK, it's the least I can do.'

'Would it be all right for us to make coffee somewhere?'

'Yes, of course. There are facilities in the church.'

'And ... um ... a few more people might need to sleep here than we'd expected ... would that be OK?'

Without thinking I replied, 'Oh, right, sure, that's fine.'

So the church was opened up, and quickly the back of the nave was transformed into a rest space for XR activists and arrestables. Chairs were placed in circles. In the corner by one of the pillars a couple of people started meditating. Before long, downstairs, in the crypt, I found people sitting and chatting, planning and murmuring between the sleeping bags and the banners. It's lucky it's Holy Week, I thought, since the orchestra is away and the theatre group is otherwise occupied. God is good.

'What are the police planning to do?' I asked.

'We don't know, yet. We've liaised with them. They knew we were coming. There are many of us who are prepared to be arrested. They may try and clear the bridge. At the moment they're just watching.'

At 5.45 p.m. I went to the back of the church and announced that we have a service at 6 p.m. for an hour and would they mind being quiet. The rebels melted away and closed the door into the crypt, and the church became silent again.

Every evening during Holy Week we follow the Stations of the Cross: the version of the last journey of Jesus from his condemnation to his burial. The first station: Jesus is condemned. Ecce homo. Behold the man. The second station: Jesus takes up his cross. Jesus falls for the first time. Jesus meets his mother. The story goes on, until he falls for the third time, is stripped of his clothes, nailed to the cross, crucified, dead, buried.

I expected there to be opposition. I foresaw anger: the church was becoming a campsite, and downstairs there was an art workshop on subversion. The congregation take good care of their building and I was girded for conflict. But when Lucia and Ester and Eileen arrived for Stations of the Cross, and when alongside them we were joined by a couple of rebels, the transition back into a place of worship was seamless.

There were reflections accompanying each station. I read them as the little group of pilgrims made its way around the church, kneeling at the appropriate moments, chanting quietly: 'Jesus, remember me, when you come into your kingdom.'

That year, I had chosen words by Oscar Romero, the Archbishop of El Salvador who was assassinated by government forces, shot while he was celebrating Mass at the altar of his cathedral in 1980. For the fifth station, Simon of Cyrene carries the cross, he wrote:

> If people want to look into their own mystery –
> the meaning of their pain,
> of their work,
> of their suffering,
> of their hope –
> let them put themselves next to Christ.
> If they accomplish what Christ accomplished –
> doing the Father's will, filling themselves with the life that
> Christ gives the world – they are fulfilling themselves as
> true human beings.[28]

For the ninth station, Jesus falls the third time, he wrote:

> The church, entrusted with the earth's glory,
> believes that each person is the Creator's image
> and that everyone who tramples it offends God.
> As holy defender of God's rights and of his images,
> the church must cry out.
> It takes as spittle in its face,
> as lashes on its back,
> as the cross in its passion,
> all that human beings suffer,
> even though they may be unbelievers.
> They suffer as God's images.[29]

I have rarely heard the crying out of the church. There has been no spittle in my face, no lashes on my back.

After we had reflected on Oscar Romero and shared in the Eucharist, I went to the crypt and told the rebels they could return. They melted back in, and the church reverted to a home for tired activists. Someone had bought biscuits. Someone else had bought oat milk. The place was quietly humming. I left by the side door, closing it quietly behind me.

In the night, the sound of sirens cut through the air. I wondered what was happening on the bridge. Early the next morning, when I went into church I found people sleeping all over the place, curled up in sleeping bags by the candle stand or in front of the altar. The place smelt of fug and exhaustion. There was a group at the back quietly drinking coffee, curled up in blankets, looking worn out but triumphant.

Amos looked every inch the prophet. His eyes were alight.

'Oh, Giles, we had a battle last night. At 3 o'clock, the police came, in their hundreds, in vans and riot gear. To clear the bridge. To arrest us all.'

'But what happened? Did you hold it?'

He smiled broadly.

'Yes! We sent out a message and reinforcements came. We kept sending more up on to the bridge. We were too many for them and in the end they gave up!'

'That's good news,' said I, wondering about my role in it all.

'About 150 people were arrested,' said Amos. 'They've been taken all over London.'

Gwendolen joined us, steaming coffee cupped in her hands.

'There was a point when we thought we wouldn't be able to hold it. But people came here to recover and then went back up. In the end the police gave up. They couldn't be nasty to us because we weren't nasty to them. We held the bridge!'

Tom was there too, looking pale as incense.

'Thank you, Father, for helping us.'

'It's the least I can do! And please call me Giles ...'

It felt good. It was the first action by Extinction Rebellion in London. They had worked out that if you want to effect change, it's best to try to be kind and generous to the people you're working with. The emergency on climate calls for drastic action. They had three demands: tell the truth; zero carbon by 2025; and a climate assembly.

When it was time for the 1 p.m. Eucharist and we needed quiet, everyone melted away again – except Graham and Katie, who came to join Eileen and Lucia, again, and Princess Elizabeth from the Bugandan royal family and me in the Lady Chapel. After the Eucharist I went up on the bridge, and wandered among the crowd. The police were there, standing around the edge. They greeted me. We chatted. They told me the policy was to contain the protest and only arrest when necessary.

Later, questions would emerge about the strategy of arrestability, and about the tactics of XR. But for now, it was humbling. The determination was palpable.

I spoke to an arrestable, again bearing a mug of coffee.

'I decided to be arrested because I realized that non-violent action on its own won't change anything. New voices have to be heard. My voice!'

'But surely,' I said, 'it'll just clog up the courts and mean that other people's trials are even more delayed?'

'Yes, there may be disruption. I'm sorry about that. But the disruption now is nothing to what will happen if we get runaway climate change. Surely you can see that? London might be uninhabitable!'

I was impressed by her quiet stubbornness. I saw her tears.

'I've never done anything like this before, Giles. It's for my grandchildren.'

After the first day, the occupation of the bridge began to settle in. There were occasional arrests. Christian Climate Action were at Marble Arch in larger numbers, praying. There was a Buddhist group meditating in the middle of the road at Oxford Circus. The congregation of St John's were being supportive. In fact they were a little proud. The rebels made friends with the Christians when they came to worship. One or two came to the Passover supper.

The conversation with Gwendolen stayed with me. It was a happy accident of the calendar that the occupation of the bridge was happening in Holy Week. We hear in the Gospel of Luke

(9.51) that Jesus, 'when the days drew near for him to be taken up, set his face to go to Jerusalem'. In the accounts of Mark, Matthew and Luke, he cleared the Temple of traders during the week of Passover – an act that, alongside his condemnations of the scribes and the Pharisees and his challenge to the religious powers of Israel, was bound to provoke a reaction. According to theologian N. T. Wright he intended the Temple clearing to be a disruptive act. He thought that only his arrest – and possibly death – would bring about the necessary change.

So, I began to say to the rebels, the arrestables are like Jesus. Extinction Rebellion is a sacrificial body trying to bring about change through deliberately transgressive acts.

'Giles, there's a man from *The Times* who wants to talk to you.'

The paper's religious affairs correspondent had found his way to St John's. We sat at the front of church in a quiet place.

'Why are you supporting these illegal acts? What difference is it going to make?'

'I'm supporting them because climate change is close to tipping point. What action has been taken by government so far isn't anywhere near enough.'

'But what about the disruption it's causing to people in London? There are ambulances not getting through, people not getting to work ...'

'Think about the disruption that will happen if we go on as we are! We're heading for catastrophe – all the science says so. Westminster and Blackfriars Bridges have been deliberately left open to allow ambulances through. And, in fact, people round here are being remarkably supportive. They can hear the voice of XR and know it's long overdue.'

'Someone told me you're comparing Extinction Rebellion activists to Jesus?'

'I am! It's quite appropriate that this is all happening in Holy Week. I think they're like Jesus because they've decided that it's necessary to be arrested, to bring about the change they know is needed.'

'Isn't that a bit blasphemous?'

'I don't think so. We're all called to be like Jesus. And, of

course, the parallel isn't exact. Not everyone should be arrested
– for lots of people, especially black and brown people, it would
be unthinkable to voluntarily give yourself up for arrest. But
there are others – I've spoken to grandmothers and grandads –
for whom it might work, as a tactic. It's worth trying, anyway.'

He looked unconvinced.

'I'm filing my copy later today. I don't know if there will be
space. I hope so.'

It's true that many of those who were willing to be arrested
had the huge advantage of being white and middle class. To
many of them, the prospect of arrest was something to be
borne, and perhaps suffered: but it was not something that
carried an existential threat, a fear, a risk to life and health. For
a young black person growing up on the estates of Lambeth
or Southwark, it is quite different. Stereotypes of criminality
do not swirl around the heads of grandmothers from Somerset
the way they do young people from Peckham. But perhaps that
strengthened the arguments of people like Gwendolen: she
could do things on behalf of those whose voices are too often
silenced – people in other countries who are experiencing the
climate crisis more directly than many people in the UK can
begin to imagine. People yet unborn.

Late at night, after the Maundy Thursday worship and the
Watch in the garden of Gethsemane, Shanon said, 'We should
go up on the bridge. You wearing your cassock.'

My cassock is black, and it has red buttons down the front,
because I am a canon. I rarely dare to go out on the streets in
it. Too weird for words. It was after 11 p.m. but the bridge
was busy. There were a few police passing the time. There were
groups of rebels and there were Londoners passing through,
some stopping to talk, some a bit the worse for wear. The
atmosphere was golden.

I was overwhelmed by the reaction we received.

'Are you the priest from the church down the road? Are you
from St John's? Thank you for everything you're doing! Thank
you! Thank you! Will you pray with me?'

One man stopped in front of me. Maybe mid-thirties. T-shirt
and shorts.

'Will you bless me?'

I stood on Waterloo Bridge on the night of Maundy Thursday and blessed a man who was preparing to spend the night in the garden they had made – a true garden bridge, a place of encounter – and who might the next day be arrested and taken to prison. Then I went home to the comfort of my bed. Hmm.

The next day I found this in *The Times*:

Protesters are like Jesus, says vicar helping to blockade bridge
A Church of England vicar played a pivotal role in sustaining Extinction Rebellion's Waterloo Bridge blockade this week by inviting the protesters to use the facilities at his nearby church. The Revd Canon Giles Goddard, who likens the protestors to Jesus in their willingness to be arrested to achieve 'necessary change' agreed three weeks ago to provide vital support to the group … Mr Goddard gave the keys to the crypt to Amos Jacob, 27, an Extinction Rebellion coordinator and freelance gardener from Falmouth in Cornwall, who said: 'It's amazing. I don't think we would have held the bridge if we didn't have it.' He said the vicar had been 'more than happy [to help]. He's grinning from ear to ear.' Mr Goddard cited Rowan Williams, the former Archbishop of Canterbury, who has publicly backed the group since it emerged in October.[30]

I was envious of Gwendolen and Amos and their cohorts. I did what I could to support them, convinced that theirs was a voice that had to be heard. The XR philosophy, when the movement began, was to mobilize at least three per cent of the population, on the basis from previous historical experience that only a small percentage of adherents in a society can be sufficient to create a tipping point. They embraced non-violence and believed in persuasion. As all movements need, they had their activists and they had their supporters. I thought of the women in the Gospels who stayed at home and made sure the itinerant disciples following Jesus had enough to eat. I wanted to be one of the disciples, not one of the people who stays at home – but in reality, even on the bleakness of Holy Saturday, almost at the end of a Holy Week I had tried to observe with great seriousness, I had to admit to myself that I was a stayer, not an adventurer.

Since that coffee with Siobhan I've worked hard on climate change. Perhaps the background support is as important as the dramatic gesture: perhaps we are all on the same spectrum. Trying to change the world, step by step. Even so, that Holy Saturday, I felt quite feeble.

23

The deepest paradox

2023

The deepest paradox of all is that life comes through death: fulfilment is achieved through sacrifice. By letting go I learn to hold on. The negation of desire gives rise to the fulfilment of desire. This is not altruism. It is self-denial in order to discover what lies beyond the self.

In 2015 I spent time in South Africa, staying in a monastery high on the Eastern Cape, and then travelled the long way home via Easter Island. The furthest point of my journey was a small island, part of the Samoan archipelago. When I arrived there the people were angry; the ferry should have stayed in port, for a cyclone was imminent. Everything was being packed away. I was given a floor in a concrete storeroom to sleep on. The risk was great, although to me it was more of an adventure than a risk, and I treated it lightly until I was brought to heel by a fellow traveller. 'Giles, this is really dangerous, we could all die.'

The cyclone changed course at the last minute, and although there were gales, no trees fell and we all survived. That evening, I went swimming in the lagoon, alone. I thought it would be fun to leave the lagoon and swim out into the open sea as the sun set, so I could look back at the palm-fringed shore where I survived a cyclone.

Leaving the lagoon was easier than getting back. I was caught in an ocean current that swept round the island and out into sea. Suddenly the idea of swimming out to sea did not feel nearly as wonderful. I did not realize how swiftly I was being swept away until I looked at the shore and saw the palm trees shrinking in the distance. I was wearing flippers; I turned, and tried to swim against the current, but it was too hard and I made no headway even with the flippers. I quickly got tired. No one knew I had gone for a swim. No one would rescue me. I remembered the recent death of the priest of a parish near me in London. He went swimming on his own on the Great Barrier Reef and was never seen again.

I remembered that I had read somewhere that to escape from a current you have to swim across it, not against it. I struck out diagonally towards the shore. I was afraid. The adrenalin gave me strength. I swam hard, and after a struggle I began to escape from the current. I headed back inland, and at last I landed on the beach and could walk back along the shore to my cabin. I was trembling. It felt like a close brush with death alone in a distant ocean.

There have been others. A moment's doze one hot afternoon when I was driving from Damascus through the Syrian desert towards Palmyra. Waking up and over-correcting so that the car spun out of control. Luckily there were no trucks coming towards us and we ended in the ditch, but the police station to which we were taken had a graveyard of smashed cars.

There have been times of foolishness. Stupid risks from which, by the grace of God, I escaped. My blood runs cold at the thought of the consequences if I had died, especially for my mother, her love poured into this replacement son. The waste of life, the waste of time. All I would have missed.

But there is another consequence to those rash moments. Similar perhaps to the feelings of people who have survived a life-threatening illness or a violent situation. I am glad to be alive in a way that I was not, before. I am grateful that blood still runs through my veins and that my heart still keeps beating, unremarked and unthanked.

I am not someone who takes risks for pleasure. I do not go free climbing or leap across the gaps between high buildings. But a safe life is an unexamined life. Risks are endemic to discovery. Another word for risk is experiment. Without experiments we do not learn. If we do not take risks we do not grow.

Taking a risk requires the decision to trust. A mountain climber, a sky diver, a trapeze artist; these people rely on others for their safety. Stepping out on to the rope between the circus poles, or scrambling up a chimney in the Himalayas, trusting that the leader is holding the line and taking the strain.

The greatest risk of all is the one we take with our hearts. If we want to protect ourselves we resist entering into relationships, for relationships entail loss and pain. Grief is the price we pay for love. Yet we take the risk. To trust ourselves to the other. Why? Because without the potential for pain we are also deprived of the potential for joy. Joy is the wage we receive for love.

My time is not your time, my truth is not your truth. My experience of time is different to yours. I am unutterably separate from the world and from the people closest to me. Beyond us and between us is an ocean of invisible matter, dark matter, something no one has either seen or touched and probably never will. We are separated by an abyss, *l'abîme*, a nothingness. But we have developed a way of communication that papers over the abyss. With a look of love. With a touch, an embrace, a caress. With a shout of laughter or a cry of pain. With a gift.

My time is not your time and yet I live as if it is. 'I am, because you are,' says the well-known Ubuntu phrase. But discovering who 'you' are also requires the discovery of who 'I' am.

We have to learn to trust. We start to learn to trust when we are very tiny. When I was an infant, I had no understanding of the world as separate from me. Before I knew how distant from me you were, before I knew my name and certainly had no idea of yours, I thought that I and the world around me were united. When I looked at you, you looked back, and when I smiled you smiled, and when I cried you came running. Shortly after that I learnt that I could form sounds in ways that sounded similar to the ways you formed sounds, and that the sounds I formed had meaning, because you understood the sound in the same way I did.

I began to find a way of communicating with you. At the time, it did not feel like a risk. It felt as if you had a role, a function, and your function was to serve me – to make sure I was full of food when I wanted food, and clean when I wanted to be clean, and asleep when I wanted to be asleep. But then I realized that my understanding of our relationship was a bit one-sided.

I discovered that I could not bend the world to suit me and that you would not automatically respond to my demands.

I had to work out how I might survive in this world that suddenly seemed arbitrary and frightening. I began to learn that life depended on trust. That I had to trust that if you said you were going to be there to collect me from school you would be. That if you said you loved me you meant it. And if I said I loved you, I had to mean that too.

You waved at me from the top of the cliff on the other side, and I waved back. I shot an arrow across, tied to a rope, and then I tied another rope to that rope, and then you shot another arrow back tied to another rope, and after a while we had a bridge. I stepped out over the abyss and made my way to the centre, hardly daring to look down, hoping to reach you before I fell. That was a risky business, to be sure. Safer, surely, to learn to walk a tightrope. To try to stand on the bridge alone. But alone is not alive. I am because we are. As the decades went by I inchingly began to learn to trust in the instinct to embrace.

But that process of learning to trust is never easy. The pain and the tragedies we face are mountains that have to be climbed. Sometimes, often, the route is not clear, and we have to ask for help to work out our path. Some sessions of counselling after the death of my father taught me much, but above all the words of the counsellor, which have stayed with me: 'Giles, you don't have to compete with a dead three-year-old.'

I had to work out how to come out of the shadow and into the sun – to become the person I knew deep down that I could become. I had to learn that darkness and grief are part of the human story too. They need space, acknowledgement, love. The brushes with death, yes, but also the other moments, the times of loneliness or loss, they are all notes in the melody we struggle to sing.

Above all, I had to dare to trust the in the power of love, the power that gives it life and strength. And to see the face of Nicholas, not leering but smiling, wishing me well as I began to learn from others how to cross the bridge.

To change is to grow, said John Henry Newman, and to be perfect is to have changed often. Every step we take is a step into a new story: art and creativity is a series of responses to the question 'What if?' The further I step out, the more I depend on the twisted strands of the rope bridge for survival, and the more I have to lose should the strands all snap. The further I step out, the more exposed I feel. But I want to tread the path wherever it leads.

I am learning to understand the correspondence between spirit and matter; between the not-now and the now, the time-less and the momentary, the infinite and the boundaried. How the bursting of the infinite into the everyday is told in different stories: Muhammad, Jesus, Mother Julian, Rumi, Giles.

I am learning about a world where everyone can touch the hem of the divine, where to live is to be fully alive, where we can all glimpse the light of desire at the end of the tunnel and allow it to draw us towards its source.

I am learning to embrace my wounds, to understand that without the hurts and the pain I would not be the person I am.

I am learning to be compassionate, holding those whose wounds are infinitely greater and more debilitating than mine.

I am learning to understand prayer and spiritual practice, the rucksack for the journey, the map, the compass, something understood.

I am learning to feel friendship, nourished over decades of journeying together or fragmentary, fleeting, sprouting for a moment in the forest until our paths diverge suddenly or slowly.

I am learning to love:

particular loves: Shanon, the congregation, my friends, my family, me
general loves: the sea in which I swim, the infinite.

24

The silent city

The sudden silence of lockdown. Streets echoing and vacant. Waterloo Station a void, no one to be seen between me and the clock, an acre of empty floor. Shops closed. The South Bank quiet, the screams of seagulls loud in my ears. A blackbird and her mate made a nest in the ivy in the garden, and Shanon and I watched as they reared first one brood and then another, returning from forays with beaks full of worms. Fear. Closed doors and closed windows.

It felt as if we all went into the ark. It felt as if the groundwork we had done, the foundations I had been laying, enabled us to move collectively from our geographical roots in the marsh of Waterloo to a network spanning thousands of miles and millions of megabytes. Andy's father lived in Johannesburg. Unexpectedly he passed away. Andy arrived in the hospital shortly after his father's death. He had to sort out the estate and to find a way to care for Leonie, his stepmother. He was stuck in Johannesburg. But he was not alone, for he joined us on Zoom on Sunday mornings. We began saying Morning Prayer online every day, and then there was a coffee morning at 11 a.m., and Andy was there at all of them. Sheila was well over 80 and found it hard to leave her house. She had been struggling to get to the 9 o'clock service in person. With help from her nephew and from Lisa, she worked out how to log on, and there she was at all our services, her camera sometimes misaligned – we can only see your ear, Sheila! – but after a while we sorted that out too. Keith went to Hertfordshire with Winifred. Tatiana's parents were in Germany. But in gallery view they were all present and correct, and in the top left-hand corner I could see myself, in a white alb and a purple stole (it was Lent) speaking to camera, praying, hearing the responses, until everyone went on mute because the time lag was too cacophonous, 'In the name of Christ, Amen!' Euchar played the piano in Walthamstow, and Georgie led the prayers in Devon.

Around us, death and destruction. Close to the ark, and sometimes within it too. Ulrike one of the first, heartbreakingly, as she had been the first to raise with me the need for precautions, back in January. It hit her hard. Joyce, too, Michaiah, the organist's wife, who is a nurse. James, from Uganda. Isabelle, the Archbishop's chaplain. The upstairs neighbour of Susan. Many died. Collectively we prayed, and we tried to offer what help we could. We kept the food bank open for as long as possible. The homeless people sleeping here as part of the Robes Project had to remain in East Dulwich at short notice, inspiring the wrath of Steve who was organizing it. But we gathered in our ones and twos and somehow the bonds that we had forged grew stronger.

I sent an email, daily, to the congregation. Here is one, chosen at random:

Dear all.
Each day feels very different to me. Today I woke up feeling anxious and sad, as the reality begins to bite and the many ways that our lives are radically disrupted become clear. I feel sad for the young people whose exams are cancelled, and anxious about how they will get the qualifications they need. I feel anxious for the traders in our Food Court who have had to shut up shop, anxious for those who have lost their jobs, and for my friend who is an anaesthetist at St Thomas'; and sad because of all the good things that are no longer happening. I feel anxious for those who are sick, and all of us as we worry about our own health.

Once again we are reminded of our human vulnerability – how fragile life is. Now is the time when our dependence on love, on God, is more clear than ever.

But I am also reminded of our human resourcefulness, and our infinite capacity to love and to transform.

The WhatsApp group is alive: let me know if you would like to join. And further details will follow very soon about the live-streamed service on Sunday. Many of us are in touch with one another. I am sure many of you are linked into other local networks as well, such as the Bishops Ward Covid Aid WhatsApp group. Please let me know if you are aware of anything further needed by anyone.

Finally a scripture verse: Are not two sparrows sold for a penny? Yet not one of them will fall to the ground unperceived by your Father. And even the hairs of your head are all counted. So do not be afraid; you are of more value than many sparrows (Matt. 10.29–31).

With my love, and much prayer,
Giles

The doorbell rings. It's New Year's Eve in the first year of the pandemic, and Luis is on the doorstep, dressed in his warm red jacket with three or four layers beneath. The churchyard is silvered by frost. Luis is wearing a mask, as he has done constantly since lockdown started. On the day we had to close he was mopping the floor of the church, and his bucket and mop remained for months in the middle of the floor, abandoned.

'Father! I have this for you and Shanon!' He places a box of Celebrations on the step. 'Happy New Year!'

Shortly afterwards, the doorbell rings again.

'Are you going clubbing?' asks Elaine, brightly. She is a churchwarden and looks after my welfare.

'No, we are *not* going clubbing. We are staying at home along with the rest of London. New Year's Eve has been cancelled.'

'I know,' she said. That's why I brought you this.' She places a bottle of champagne on the step. 'Happy New Year!'

It turns out indeed to be a happy New Year. The WhatsApp group is lively with the exchange of ideas and jokes. Anton has asked whether anyone has a favourite book from 2020. Shanon has created a playlist with Christmas tunes from across the world, all suggested by members of the congregation: 'Hark the herald angels sing', suggested by David, 'Woulida L Masih

Halleluia', nominated by Nader, and 'The rebel Jesus' put forward by Veronica.

All our services are on Zoom. I start the meeting and people pop up from all over the place, listening, reflecting, praying. Francoise was there, from the comfort of her living room in South East London. So was Joshua, from Lancashire, aged 19, thinking of ordination. So was Nancy, tempted in by something, she knew not what, wanting to find a way to speak of God in spite of her perception of the church as homophobic and unwelcoming. And Ulrike's mum and dad join from near Frankfurt.

I look at the screen of the church laptop and see 50 people, in tiny close-up, all gathering online to perform the counter-intuitive ritual of the consecration of bread and wine so that it will, in some sense, become the body and blood of the God who, in some sense, became human at a specific time in a specific place now quarrelled over and besmirched by blood and death. Why do they gather, especially now, when the ceremony is at such a distant remove from the traditional reality – when the people may not eat or drink, but only watch from afar the priest eating and drinking, locked in the sanctuary?

Eileen read the first reading, from the book of the prophet Isaiah.

> The people who walked in darkness
>   have seen a great light;
> those who lived in a land of deep darkness –
>   on them the light has shined. (Isa. 9.2)

Those optimistic words resonate down the millennia. As I listened I remembered the picture of the prophet painted by Raphael on the wall of the church of San Domenico in Rome, just across the aisle from the great triptych of the calling and martyrdom of St Matthew by Caravaggio. Matthew in his tax-collector's office, surrounded by other men. I had always assumed that the bearded older figure was the disciple being called, the tender eyes of Jesus lighting upon him. But, looking again at the picture, it is hard to see where Jesus' gaze lies, and each person in the picture could be the one being called into a different life.

It feels mediaeval, like the period when the priest spoke in Latin, high up the chancel, far away from the congregation. While he muttered away incomprehensibly they carried on with their orisons, visiting chapel after chapel, seeking the succour and help of the saints around them, until suddenly at the moment of consecration the bells were rung and the priest (his back to the congregation, facing upwards and outwards towards the transcendent God) would lift the host high above his head so that the congregation could see it – 'Higher, friend, higher!' might come the shout from the nave if the talismanic view was obscured or if the priest was half-hearted in his lifting. And forward they would shuffle, one by one, to receive the bread on the tongue, no words, only the symbol, before they returned to their intercessions and their imprecations on their way out into the fields to hoe or plough. And here, now, I am in the church on Zoom and there in their living rooms and kitchens are the congregation, watching, listening, singing (all on mute) and participating, at a distance twice removed, in this ancient rite of which I know not the meaning, and neither do they, and yet back they come, week after week, albeit with doubts and questions, believing that this is the thing that gives meaning to their lives.

We could have been in a situation so much worse. I shared my fears and my hopes with the congregation. I was as open and vulnerable as I could be, wanting everyone to be aware that we are all in the same boat (although, as it turned out later, we weren't, and the (mainly black) health workers in the congregation already knew how disproportionately vulnerable they were). I learnt, over and over again, of quiet acts of love that happened locally and internationally. Winifred, the long-retired PA to the Sierra Leonian High Commissioner, was supported by Nicola and Paul, who lived above her; they left a printed copy of the service for her so that she could join by phone. Jenny was fulfilling her task, making sure the churchyard was watered. Morning Prayer online brought together people all over the world.

I became even more sure that the reality that underlies all others is love. Love as an actual force, love as more than a metaphor, love as something tangible and testable, love as the London clay upon which our (now closed) building rests.

New people came to us. John Godpower Deeny, Manon Mathis. We drew them in. We tried to build a new home, a house built on rock, a spiritual home in the midst of intense levels of uncertainty. The proximity of death. I asked Shanon to make his will, and checked that mine was in order.

Silence in the city. The soft sound of wind in trees. The lonely call of the curlew whispering beneath the silence of the new normal. Wildness below us and all around us as we walked along the deserted paths by the river.

And, somehow, the enchantment. Thinking of John de Colon, my predecessor confronting the Black Death in 1348, I was more aware than ever of the porosity of the boundaries between the temporal and the eternal, holes rent in the fabric of time. Bonds connected us across the world, the sudden miracle of Zoom, and it was all given sharp relief by the vision that held us together, the online silence after communion had been distributed, those moments heavy with meaning where unconditional love could be inhaled, a joyful miasma amid the airborne fear.

The pandemic gave me time to think, and to pray. Shanon and I started yoga, doing half an hour every day. Before the pandemic, he had joined a couple of silent Sufi meditations from the Naqshbandi order – in Kuala Lumpur and London – which practised total silence lasting 40 to 50 minutes. We expanded our practice from 10 to 40 minutes, and the silence expanded to fit the space available. I prayed for the carers and the hospital workers among us. Around me I felt the breath of ghosts who had suffered, cried and lived lives as fragile as ours.

The fragility was exacerbated by the torrent of bad environmental news that we read in the hours between yoga and meditation. The Age of Extinction. The melting of the ice sheets. Acidification of the oceans, lakesful of plastic, drought and tempest and cyclone. This year was to be a Year of Climate Action as the COP circus came to Glasgow, and we were gearing up for a massive push on climate, the network I had founded, Faith for the Climate, taking a wider role as it tried to pull together all those different faith groups – Buddhist-Muslim-Hindu-Jewish-Jain-Bahai-Christian-Zoroastrian-Pagan – unfurling a strategy to ensure that the thousands of members of faith groups across the country could take action to try to reverse the progress of global heating and make their voices heard in the corridors where life-and-death decisions were being made. But everything was put on hold, and although carbon output shrunk dramatically, we read that the reduction was nowhere like enough to reverse global heating.

Lambeth, an epicentre for infection, all of us suddenly epidemiologists. All of us staying indoors. The church's doors closed. The mop in a bucket left in the middle of the floor. No church services on Sunday, for the first time since the church was opened in 1824. Everyone banned from the building, even Eileen. Fear. How are you feeling, who do you know who has had it? I went for a walk, just before lockdown, with Kurt, a doctor. Right at the start, he went down with Covid, along with many of his colleagues. He emailed me and Shanon to say we must be tested, and he organized it, and we were negative. But the illness took hold and after a few days I stopped hearing from him. I emailed him and received no reply. After a few days I was afraid he'd died. I wrote again, hoping for a response, afraid I might not receive one. There was a night when he looked at his clock each hour, and gave thanks that he had made it through another hour. He prepared for his death. His fragility, his life on a thread. He survived, just. But for weeks afterwards he was weakened and could hardly walk.

The second wave of Covid swept across London. Francoise was working back in London. Once again she came to see me; we sat, socially distanced, on either side of the table in the garden. Her hospital specializes in provision for people with mental health issues. Locked wards hold people with severe behavioural challenges or cognitive impairment.

'How can we explain lockdown and the need for social distancing to our patients?' she asks. 'They just don't understand. We have to tell them over and over again. There is someone who insists on hugging everyone. How can we stop her? And there's sometimes violence. It's scary, Giles. It feels dark. A patient took his own life. He was on day release. He threw himself under a train. He was distressed. Upset. Out of control.' She looks away and I can see her trying not to cry. She is contained. It hurts to listen. The thought of the locked wards, the infection spreading, Francoise in her white coat trying to make sense of it all.

'And where is God in all this?' she goes on. 'It's exhausting. I am completely worn out. Sometimes I can barely get home.'

That question over and over again. And behind it: what's the point of having faith, in a world so damaged and broken?

Shanon and I went for a midnight walk, on the night before New Year. We took the quiet back streets from here towards London Bridge, following the ancient street patterns. Roupell Street still pretty much as it was when it was built for railway workers, destroying Colonel Astley's circus ring. Mr Roupell built it back in the 1820s. The street was dust and dirt then, but the front doorsteps were kept immaculate by the women of the houses, and there was a school at the end of the street provided by St Andrew's Church for the poor children of the tenements. Today, Teslas and BMWs line the tarmacked street, except at weekends when they slide or purr away to the countryside.

We walked in the lockdown quiet. We half-closed our eyes and imagined the figures of the past crowding the pavements. We glimpsed Charles Dickens on one of his night walks, listening and touching the sounds and sights of a cruelly divided London. He might well have wandered across Blackfriars Bridge and veered left into the warren of alleys behind the river, where the Bishop of Winchester had kept brothels and lived on the income from the rents. The remnants of the Bishop's Palace are still there, surrounded by warehouses and offices and the high quality comestibles of Borough Market. Enduja and oysters for the delectation of the finer classes.

'Look!' I say. 'Over there, can you see it?'

'What?'

'That mysterious grey form, coming towards us! Hide, quick!'

'Shut up, Giles. Don't joke about the spirits!'

We were off to the haunts of the dead, to see if on this last night of a difficult year the spirits were stirring. We came to a high wall surrounding an ancient graveyard. Along Redcross Way are the gates to the cemetery: wide, closed, locked, and festooned with ribbons and charms and photographs of the dead.

Crossbones Graveyard was in use from the eleventh century until 1854. It is believed to have been the unconsecrated ground wherein people who died without having made their confession were buried, outside the arms of the church. It is believed to have been the place where sex workers, the Bishop of Winchester's chickens, were laid to their final rest. It has become a place where the vulnerable and the marginal are remembered. The sex worker victims of the Essex murderer have ribbons dedicated to them. Faded laminated black and white photographs of homeless people have been tied to the railings, and someone has threaded flowers through the bars of the gates, which are now desiccated and dead.

The moon was full. Shanon peered at the noticeboards. I squinted through the gates between the fading ribbons and saw a shadowy statue of the Virgin Mary. I thought of the phalanxes of people who have passed through these gates, bringing the corpses of the dead to be interred for all eternity. Generations have passed along these streets since they were all owned by the Abbey of Bermondsey. Above us, the Shard was pointing towards heaven in its Christmas finery. A corner of London, victim and beneficiary of the power of commerce.

25

Is there anybody there?

2022

The echoes of the tragedy still resonate 60 years after Nicholas fell in the pond. If only I could say, 'With one bound, I was free', but these things are never simple. Patterns of behaviour, once established, are hard to change. It is hard to learn to love, truly, when you have no love for yourself. As the great Ru Paul says, 'If you can't even love yourself, how in hell are you going to learn to love somebody else? Can I get an Amen for that? Let the music play!'

Imagine then that the child had not drowned. Imagine that my parents had patched up their relationship, and they went on to have two more children, Delia and Giles, but instead of Giles being the inadequate replacement for a dead three-year-old he was the younger brother of a delightful and charming son of the shires, who took care of him as necessary and bullied him appropriately. Giles was alone, sometimes, to be sure – but the alliances in the family were not the girls together and Giles on his own, but Katie and Nicholas together and Delia and Giles together. Imagine that Giles had the confidence from the start to be who he wanted to be. To trust in the person he knew he could be. Imagine that Nicholas realized early on that Giles was gay and thought nothing of it. Imagine that Giles still had his passion for justice and his sense of being an outsider, but that alongside that was a sense of himself as someone desirable and worthy of attention, not a disappointment when measured, even subconsciously, against his dead brother.

Just imagine.

Our mother is in a care home now. She had to go there when she could no longer care for herself. As she has grown older, her anger at the world around her has become more unfiltered. She cannot understand why she is there.

'I could manage perfectly well at home. I don't need all these people around. You've just put me here because it's easier for you.' My sisters and I dread the visits, not knowing what reception we'll receive when we walk into her room, which overlooks the marshes and the river behind Aldeburgh.

Katie and I arrived one Friday morning.

'We're going to take you out.'

'Must we?'

After a struggle she was dressed and in the car. We headed to the forest. A summer's day, a burning heatwave in July 2022 prefiguring catastrophic climate change. The forest was dark, overshadowed, conifers creating pathways threaded with treacherous roots. A supposedly accessible trail for wheelchairs turned out to be full of traps. In the shade when the sun was behind cloud it was cool.

'Goodness, I'm cold.'

But there came a clearing where a tree had fallen, fresh green grass, pink rosebay willowherb, the tweeting of a blue tit somewhere in the trees beside us. We stopped. Mum in her wheelchair. Katie and I sitting on the grass beside her.

A sudden memory, from childhood. Mum and I in the sitting room. Talking about the war. The air raids. She was still at school, at the Royal Naval College. 'The headmistress said that officers' daughters didn't evacuate,' she had told me. 'So we stayed in London while the bombs fell around us. I was terrified. I used to comfort myself by quoting a poem.'

I remembered the poem she had told me about and began to quote it.

'Is there anybody there?' said the Traveller,
Knocking on the moonlit door;
And his horse, in the silence, champed the grasses
Of the forest's ferny floor.[31]

Mum looked at me.

'I know that poem,' she said. 'I remember it!'

'You used to quote it during air raids,'

'Did I? Did I tell you that?'

'Yes. Can you remember how it goes on?' Quickly I found it on my phone.

And a bird flew up out of the turret,
Above the Traveller's head:
And he smote upon the door again a second time;
'Is there anybody there?' he said.
But no one descended to the Traveller;
No head from the leaf-fringed sill ...

'No head from the leaf-fringed sill,' broke in Mum. 'Leaned over and looked into his grey eyes, where he stood, perplexed and still.'

'Where he stood, perplexed and still,' said Katie. 'Perplexed. Such a good word.'

'No head from the leaf-fringed sill,' said Mum. 'I remember that. Did I really quote it during air raids?'

'That's what you said.'

I looked up and saw the expression on her face. Suddenly softer, a smile in the sunshine.

'No head from the leaf-fringed sill,' she mused, 'Leaned over and looked into his grey eyes, Where he stood, perplexed and still.'

We had the poem again, a second time, and then again.

'Tell them I came, and no one answered.
That I kept my word,' he said.

She remembered most of if, in the end. The silence surging softly backward, when the plunging hoofs were gone.

After a while we were quiet, and her face held a reverie. After another while, a cloud came over the sun and it was time to go back. In the car, after we had dropped her off, the saying good-bye was surprisingly easy.

'That was a moment, wasn't it,' Katie said.

'Something to remember,' I said. 'I'm grateful.'

26

Say his name

2020

In the middle of the pandemic, George Floyd was murdered. The picture over and over again of the black man under the heel of the white policeman. I can't breathe. I can't breathe. I can't breathe. Sickness in our hearts and our stomachs. The video in its remorseless honesty. The man dead on the street corner in the city deep in the Midwest, his death a touchpaper for something that changed the shape of everything.

Suddenly no one could deny what they had suspected or refused to acknowledge before. The knee on the neck, the powerlessness, the deaths. The revulsion. Shanon and Donna and Laych and I went to the protest. Twenty thousand people, over half black, over half young, all wearing masks, many bearing banners. The square was very full, people packed together despite Covid. There was no sound system, no great line-up of speakers. It was a demonstration unlike any I had been to before, and I have been to many: Section 28, Pride, Support the Miners, pro Palestine, anti Brexit, against the Church Commissioners' sale of housing locally. Always lots of people like me. BLM was not people like me. Lots of young people, all masked. Black Lives Matter! Black Lives Matter! Say his name! George Floyd! Say his name! George Floyd! The right-wing press attacked them for not social distancing during Covid. There was no infection spike after the BLM protests. There was passion, and hurt, and fear, and hope. We carried banners on behalf of Melba who was at home looking after Dominic, her one-year old. My life matters! Dell was there with his children, Lola and Ella. The sun shone over Parliament Square: and it shone later that month, in Brockwell Park, when churches together in South Lambeth came together in prayer and protest. We took the knee. Alongside. Solidarity.

I remembered the outpourings of wrath at previous demonstrations, which had felt so powerful but seeped away into the sand. A million people marching against the Iraq war, a million people marching against Brexit, and nothing changed. I was afraid that the support for the BLM protests was really about Covid and lockdown and frustration and isolation and that the protests might seep away.

The power of an image. The little Syrian boy, Aylan Kurdi, lying face down on the beach, water lapping over him, his red t-shirt, his blue shorts. The same age as my brother Nicholas, lying face down in the pond in my grandmother's garden. J. M. W. Turner's picture of the slave ship. Fish feasting on the slaves thrown overboard.

That image of George Floyd staring at the camera can never be eradicated and everyone who has seen it will never forget it. For me, a privileged white man in a privileged country, the story was a challenge. I had tried to say the right things about racism and power but, viscerally, I was part of the problem. I scarcely knew the language to use to enable myself to retell the story.

I am complicit. My sense of entitlement carries me through. My grandmother's comfortably large house in Sussex contained, in the children's playroom, a copy of a book called *Little Black Sambo*. When I was a child, I read it often and I remember its pictures today.

The Church of England takes its place in history very seriously: it has a long life, as an institution, and one of its pre-eminent objectives is to pass on the faith to future generations, which means it must be robust, and resilient, and hang on to the power and the influence it has. Part of my task, as vicar of a parish, is to preserve the parish in a good state so that it can be handed on well to the next generation. My role is to conserve, and not, therefore, to rock the boat too much. I have been complicit in the retention of traditional power structures, for the sake, I told myself, of strengthening the institution.

But not always. At St Peter's, early on in my time there, a vacancy occurred for churchwarden. I suggested in a sermon that it would be good if the vacancy could be filled by a black person. Immediately after the service, Toro came forward. 'I would like to be churchwarden.' Tall, Nigerian, elegant, thoughtful, hardworking. She was duly elected, and retained the role for six years, and was wonderful. Similarly, at St John's, a vacancy occurred. This time, Alice came forward, from the Ugandan community. Quiet, resilient, careful, aware, with her five wonderful children and her staunch husband Roy. She and Belinda made a dream churchwardens team.

It is not enough. These things are manifestations of a deeper malaise, which Black Lives Matter made me analyse more deeply. Having Shanon in the house helped, with his trenchant analysis of power and marginalization. I read books – notably *The Black Christ* by Kelly Brown Douglas, and Reni Eddo-Lodge's *Why I am No Longer Talking to White People about Race*. My own life experience was unavoidable – I have a history of mis-directed relationships with black people, which brings me a huge amount of guilt.

There is a dynamic tension within Christianity; the urge for reform struggles against the conservative drag. Jesus stood up in the synagogue and unrolled the scroll and read:

'The Spirit of the Lord is upon me,
  because he has anointed me
    to bring good news to the poor.
He has sent me to proclaim release to the captives
  and recovery of sight to the blind,
    to let the oppressed go free,
to proclaim the year of the Lord's favour.' (Luke 4.18–19)

I can't breathe. There in our masks, our breathing obstructed, we stood alongside one another, young black people in groups, older white people well meaning and determined. It felt like a place of friendship. 'There is no longer Jew or Greek, there is no longer slave or free, there is no longer male or female, for all of you are one in Christ Jesus' (Gal. 3.28).

I try now to look into the eyes of the person to whom I am speaking. Past the colour of their skin, past their age, past their wealth, past their health. I try to listen to the timbre of their voice, not their accent or their grammar. I try to feel the reaching out of their heart to mine, finding its way through my labyrinth of feelings, through the guilt and the shame and the over-compensating laughter and the voices deep within me manifesting ingrained prejudices.

There are the deepest connections between racism, sexism and homophobia. All have the same underlying consequence. People are denied their full humanity. People are told, subtly or blatantly, that their existence is unwelcome or is inadequate. The damage done is unquantifiable; verbal and physical abuse, beatings, murder. A just society is a society where everyone is equally valued. Where each of us can say, without fear or shame, this is me. Where we can say our names and know that we are safe, and home, and loved.

27

ReIGNITE

Light. As the scaffolding begins to come down, the space is flooded with a new kind of light. Something we had barely believed possible. New glass in the windows allows the sun to stream through, brightening the new sculptural forms Eric designed to embrace the altar and the sanctuary. He and James have chosen the most delicate of whites and greys to lift the space, and the sun plays with shadows creating a new sense of bright and dark. To the right and left of the altar, deep purple and deep green panels reflect the liturgical seasons of Advent, Lent and Ordinary Time. Newly carved seating in fine oak adds to the beauty, and above it all hangs the resurrected picture of Christ crucified, re-brightened by Claudia, our restorer. Its newly revealed colours pop across the space, resonating with the carefully created palate that shines the church into warmth.

The church is filling up. Everyone who has played a part in the project is there: architects and builders and engineers and fundraisers, and David the project manager, and the Arch-deacon, all gathering for the great service of rededication. The Archbishop arrives, and I meet him on the steps.

'When are you starting the renovation, Giles?'

'Ha! Very funny!'

The organ has been brought back to life after a year of moth-balling. The choir is resurrected and is seated finely where it always sat, to the right of the altar. My sister and her husband have arrived and are sitting with my friend Robin. Other friends from university days and the decades since are present. Many from Okusinza have come in their Ugandan finery bringing flashes of crimson, vermilion and viridian to the scene. There is a quiet delight, and a sense of achievement – hard won, for the building works overran, mainly because of the asbestos, and to keep to anything like the original schedule for reopening has been a huge struggle. Hard won, too, for asbestos knocked the budget for six, and we have had to duck and dive to make the whole thing work financially.

No matter. We are there, now, and there is great expectation. Archbishop Justin robes along with the Bishop of Kingston and the Archdeacon and me and Georgia, our new curate, and the serving team. He has brought a special chasuble of white and flame-gold for the celebration, and a white mitre. Together we bring the cross to the main doors, which have been closed.

As the doors are opened, the westward sun floods through, and there, silhouetted against the sun, stand the Archbishop with his mitre and Elaine and Faye flanking him, each bearing their churchwarden's wand.

Euchar has written a fanfare. Trumpets sound through the church, and then the organ strikes up the first hymn, and we process, joyfully, through the congregation, singing.

> The Church's one foundation
> is Jesus Christ, her Lord;
> she is his new creation
> by water and the word:
> from heav'n he came and sought her
> to be his holy bride;
> with his own blood he bought her,
> and for her life he died.[32]

The service begins. Ester, representing Okusinza mu Luganda, reads the first reading, from the First Letter of Peter.

> But you are a chosen race, a royal priesthood, a holy nation, God's own people, in order that you may proclaim the mighty acts of him who called you out of darkness into his marvellous light. (1 Pet. 2.9)

The Archbishop uses this as the text for his sermon. He'd thought hard about what he was going to say, and what he does say brings together the work of the renovation with the work of the congregation in a way that both encourages and challenges.

> In our church history, we find people who say, 'Put up a wall, keep the unholy separate.' But that is not what Peter says. He says, 'Go out, engage, transform.' We are to declare the wonderful works of God. Jesus's incarnation, and life and death, and resurrection and ascension and the sending of the Holy Spirit into an unholy world shows that separation is not the same as holiness.
>
> And so reflect, how do we walk together with those who are alien and exiled? What would our communion, our church around the world, the Christian church look like if everyone was loved as a chosen person of God? What would the world be like?
>
> It would put people at the centre of policy and planning; sacrifice and service at the centre of politics; life and love at the centre of community.
>
> Supremely it would put a holy God in the middle of all that we do and say. It would be a Kingdom of God, a holy place of abundance. It would be the place of dreams made real and the steps towards that are the hard ones of people changing, of communities living, of churches being generous and outward looking, of the practical life of new buildings for a new future.
>
> May God bless and strengthen you.

Holy Communion follows. Standing behind the altar Justin raises his arms in greeting to the congregation:

> The Lord be with you.
> **And also with you!**

His chasuble seems to light up like fire, completing the scene.

I am bearing the chalice. Many of the people who receive the wine catch my eye. Their smiles and greetings tell me that our rainbow congregation is happy.

Afterwards we all drink fizz, and I hear the comments on the transformation, and they are very good. The improved acoustics in the beautiful white and gold ceiling help the building to speak with a clearer voice. The new sculptures embrace the space with a pair of comforting arms. The brickwork on the crypt creates beauty in a series of meeting rooms. The front door has been opened on to the street so that refugees, asylum seekers, people seeking employment, worshippers and banqueters and concert-goers will be able to flood the place. The building has been insulated and damp-proofed and there are solar panels on the roof creating electricity to heat the crypt. This tired and shabby building has been given a new and sustainable lease of life. It has sprung back into being. Two hundred years after its birth, it is reignited, and the community is refreshed inside and around it. Time upon time, light upon light.

'It's wonderful,' says Belinda. 'Amazing. Everything we hoped for, and more. We did it, Giles. We built on the past and created a new future!'

'It was a team effort,' said I. 'And none of it would have happened without all those hours of prayer ...'

'It was indeed a team effort. And all the work and all the funding and all the heartache was worth it. Every minute.'

'The question is,' say I, 'what happens now? Now that we have these spaces, what do we do with them? As Justin said: what could it look like if everyone is loved as a chosen person of God?'

'Yes, that's our challenge,' says David. 'On this great journey – what happens next?'

28

The call of the curlew

'It's starting to make sense,' said Francoise. 'After all these years. You know I've been coming to St John's for over ten years now?'

'I hadn't realized it was so long!' I said. 'We've seen a lot of changes, haven't we?'

'Yes. In some ways. People have moved on, or passed away. Others have arrived. I think perhaps the congregation is a bit younger. But there's something else, too.'

'Go on.'

'I never intended to make this my church. I thought when I left the student accommodation next door I'd move on as well. But something has kept drawing me back. It's been a surprise, really.' She paused. She's as quiet as she ever was, and so I waited for her to continue. 'It's not just the way people have supported me through the various crises I've had, although of course that's been super helpful.'

'What else is it?'

We were in the vicarage, drinking the obligatory tea and eating the obligatory biscuits.

'I think it's something to do with the way the congregation works. That people seem genuinely to care for one another. But there's more than that. There's also a sense that we're doing it together. Take Nicola. She has a really full life doing all the things she does, but I know that she's there for us too, always wanting to see how she can help. And it's not just her – it's Mark, and Alice, and Shanon, and Eileen, and Faye ... I'm not going to list them all, but you know what I mean, don't you?'

'Did you know', I said, 'that the congregation have contributed over £1 million to ReIGNITE? Some have given a lot, others a little, but if you add it all up, that's where you get to.'

'I didn't know that,' she said. 'It's an amazing figure. But I'm not surprised. I think they have a feeling that they want to make a difference. A real difference. And that it matters. That's what's kept me coming.' She looked at me expectantly. I wasn't sure what she wanted me to say. But I found myself opening up.

'I know exactly what you mean. It's made a difference to me, too. In all sorts of ways. I think I've tried hard to make sure that people can trust one another. Too often in these small communities you hear of backbiting and gossip and mistrust. I've always hated that and tried not to let it happen. But underneath that is something else ... I think I've ...' I stopped to gather my thoughts. It was her turn to wait. 'I think I've begun to believe that I can trust who I am too, which seems to enable other people to trust who they are. I've found I can allow my fears and my fragilities to show, as well as the confidence and vision. There's something about trying to be the authentic self I am, and through that, as one of the community leaders, enabling everyone else to be their authentic selves. Does that make sense too?'

She looked a little perplexed.

'Haven't you always been your authentic self?'

'No, not fully,' I said. 'Back then, when you started coming, I hadn't integrated all the different bits of me. There was still the careerist self and the London gay self and the praying self and the unloving self and the preaching self, and they didn't speak to each other very much. I tried to keep them separate, and tried to pretend that everything was fine, when it wasn't. Being part of this community has changed all that. I think Covid helped, bizarrely; we were thrown back on our own resources. But it's more than that. I think it's been the trust and faith of people like you that has made a difference. It's meant I was able to say with confidence: "This is me."'

I'd never spoken so openly to Francoise, and I think she was as surprised as I was. But she rolled with it.

'We can't do it alone, can we?'

'You mean, without prayer?'

'Not exactly, though of course that's important. I mean, without other people. Without the congregation. We carry one another. Living in community, trying to share a rule of life, or just having a laugh together.'

'I've had to learn that it's OK to allow myself to be vulnerable. To embrace the pain, knowing that it can be transformed by the way we live, by the relationships around me. Isn't that what love is?'

'I guess so,' she said. 'It makes me think of the early church, those disciples, supporting one another after the resurrection. They must have had no idea at all of what they were doing – and yet, out of all that came all this!' She gestured towards the church building.

'Yes,' I said. 'And right at the heart of those first disciples' experience was Good Friday and Easter Day. God entering into human darkness – not denying it – and changing it for good. They had to work out what that meant. Hope. That's the journey we, too, have taken together. Not just us, either – churches and mosques and temples and climate action groups across the world are doing something similar. What we're doing is only one tiny corner of the vineyard. But for me,' I said and stopped again ...

'And for me too ... ' she said.

'It's been a privilege. I think I've learnt to understand things I never thought I'd understand – in fact I think I've learnt to understand things I never knew existed. That sense of joy and hope. You just can't do it alone.'

2019

When we arrived, the church was shining. Shanon and I had sent out a message: 'Wear bright clothes.' Our guests had taken us at our word. My sister Katie wore a scarlet hat and jacket. Melba's Ugandan tunic was sun-bright orange. Donna's dress was pistachio. Shanon and I had decided to compromise on costume: we settled for India, as his paternal grandparents were from pre-partition India before they began a new life in Malaysia, and my ancestors colonized it, so we wore gold and black shirwanis with crimson scarves and golden turbans.

We had elected to enter into a civil partnership, because of the Church of England's current position. We had been to Lambeth Town Hall and completed the formalities. That was done, and it was lovely – but today was the real celebration. As we walked into church Shanon started crying. We had asked Michaiah to play 'The Arrival of the Queen of Sheba', and as we went up the aisle, preceded by Bernhard who had agreed to officiate for the Christian bit, and Halima from Inclusive Mosque for the Muslim bit, I was conscious of the rainbow around me, the music above me and Shanon sniffling next to me.

My heart was full. We arrived at the front, and took our places. Bernhard and Halima welcomed the congregation, drawn from all the continents, church members, family, friends, out in force, over 300 people there in total, all smiling. We started the hymn:

Lord, for the years your love has kept and guided,
urged and inspired us, cheered us on our way,
sought us and saved us, pardoned and provided:
Lord of the years, we bring our thanks today.[33]

While we sang I wondered at the orchids that cascaded around the altar, the deepest purple I had ever seen, and I listened to Shanon crying and singing simultaneously, and I beamed at my family and all our friends around us.

Readings followed, from the Qur'an and the Bible – read by Naeem, Shanon's friend from Bolton, and Zoë, one of my beautiful nieces. Halima spoke, Bernhard spoke, we sang again, 'Love divine, all loves excelling' – and then came the vows. We stood at the centre of the church and, looking into Shanon's eyes, I said:

I give myself to you without reserve. I love you, trust you, and delight in you. I will share your burdens and your joys. I will go with you wherever God calls us, sharing my love and my life, my wholeness and my brokenness, my success and my failures. This is my solemn promise.

He replied, in the same words. There was an exchange of rings, there was a kiss, and there was a huge round of applause. There was a blessing, more music, laughter, cake, champagne; and afterwards there was Malaysian food, rendang and nasi lemak and rice and English wine, speeches, dancing and delight.

Matilda, another niece, looked at the party, the multi-hued guests doing a Bollywood number. Bernhard dancing in his cassock as though his life depended on it.

'This room feels like the solution to the world's problems,' she said.

My mother smiled as she was taken home. At the end of the evening, Shanon and I were seen off the premises by Naeem and Tawseef and Halima. They blessed a jug of water and passed it round so we could all drink from the same cup. Our families of choice and relationship gathered around to wave us off as we took a taxi, still resplendent in our shirwanis, to a Georgian hotel in Shoreditch. We slept the deepest sleep of happiness and love and woke to the most delicious scrambled eggs ever.

Not long after our service, Shanon and I took the Jubilee Line to West Ham and then the Overground to Purfleet, where we followed signs for the RSPB reserve on Rainham Marshes. The marshes are grey, flat, abundant. They were a military training ground for a century, left untouched by farm or developer. When they were decommissioned the RSPB bought them and set about restoring them to their pre-industrial state. An electrified fence keeps out foxes and stoats, and within the fence are lakes and scrapes, reedbeds, marsh, meadows and woodland. The rustling reeds conceal twittering warblers. There are hides into which Shanon and I went. We perched on the seats and peered through our binoculars trying to identify the birds we saw.

Some were easy. Look, a merganser, proud with his ruff. And look, flapping lazily, a marsh harrier quartering the land, hunting for voles and frogs. And look! There with an upturned bill, it's an avocet, so beautiful, so elegant in black and white.

Some were hard to identify. That little brown thing – is it a reed or a Cetti's or a marsh warbler? Really they all look the same. Perhaps it doesn't matter – because – Shanon – look over there, on the mud, at the edge of that lake! There it is, a curlew, high stepping, its bill curving down towards the earth. It's taking flight, high above the reeds, listen to its call, Shanon, at last, after all these years, the bubbling call, the sound of aeons, here again by the side of the river.

Sun shines over the city and curlews take flight, whistling across the marsh.

Acknowledgements

'The Listeners' by Walter de la Mare is quoted by kind permission of the author's Estate and the Society of Authors.

This book has been long in gestation. It started life as something more sprawling, with much more theology, and many people have helped me to bring it to this final form.

I'm grateful to Francis Spufford and all the students on the Goldsmiths MA in Creative and Life Writing; and to all who have read the various drafts and commented on them, especially Kylie Fitzpatrick, Jo Bailey Wells, Richard Cheetham, Maria Lobo and Julie Dunstan.

Huge thanks to Christine Smith and all at Canterbury Press for nursing the book to fruition.

Without the congregation of St John's in all its delightful diversity none of this could have happened: I am deeply thankful to everyone who has been part of our shared life.

Thanks to my sisters, Katie and Delia, for their calm and constant friendship.

Shanon has been a thoughtful, challenging, enlightening and unresting presence from my first ideas to the final version. Thank you, Shanon, for reading endless drafts, for the last 14 years, and for all that is to come.

References

1 Rabanus Maurus (attributed), 'Come, Holy Ghost, our souls inspire', trans. John Cosin, 1627.

2 *Common Worship: Services and Prayers for the Church of England*, The Archbishops' Council of the Church of England, London: Church House Publishing, 2000.

3 John Francis Wade (1711–86), 'O come, all ye faithful'.

4 *Common Worship: Holy Week and Easter*, The Archbishops' Council of the Church of England, London: Church House Publishing, 2010.

5 John Keble, 'New every morning is the love', 1822.

6 The Collect for Ash Wednesday, *Common Worship: Services and Prayers for the Church of England*, The Archbishops' Council of the Church of England, London: Church House Publishing, 2000.

7 The Litany, *Common Worship: Daily Prayer*, The Archbishops' Council of the Church of England, London: Church House Publishing, 2011.

8 Henri David Thoreau, *Civil Disobedience and Other Essays*, 1849.

9 Gerard Manley Hopkins, 'No worst, there is none. Pitched past pitch of Grief', *Poems and Prose*, London: Penguin Classics, 1985.

10 *Common Worship: Holy Week and Easter*.

11 Emily Dickinson (1830–86), 'To Make a Prairie'.

12 William Blake (1751–1827), 'The Little Black Boy'.

13 Eugene O'Neill, *The Great God Brown* (1926), Act 4, Scene 1.

14 *Common Worship: Holy Week and Easter*.

15 Theodulf, Bishop of Orléans (c. 820), 'All glory, laud, and honour', trans. J. M. Neale, 1854.

16 Samuel Crossman (1623–83), 'My song is love unknown'.

17 Thomas, Aquinas (1225–74), 'Of the glorious body telling', trans. J. M. Neale, 1854.

18 Isaac Watts (1674–1748), 'When I survey the wondrous cross'.

19 *Common Worship: Holy Week and Easter*.

20 Francis Spufford, *Unapologetic: Why, Despite Everything, Christianity Can Still Make Surprising Emotional Sense*, London: Canongate, 2012.

21 Faithless, 'God is a DJ', on the album, *Sunday 8PM* © 1998, Cheeky Records Ltd.

22 From The Exsultet, or Easter Proclamation.

23 St Augustine of Hippo (354-430), *Confessions*, Book 1.

24 *The Book of Common Prayer* (1662).

25 *Marriage and Same-Sex Relationships after the Shared Conversations: A Report from the House of Bishops*, GS2055, 27 January 2017.

26 *Living in Love and Faith*, https://www.churchofengland.org/resources/living-love-and-faith (accessed 13.02.2024).

27 Verse 256 of Al-Baqara, the second and longest chapter of the Qur'an.

28 Oscar Romero, *The Violence of Love*, Maryknoll, NY: Orbis Books, 2021.

29 Romero, *The Violence of Love*.

30 *The Times*, Saturday 20 April 2019.

31 Walter de la Mare, 'The Listeners', *The Collected Poems of Walter de la Mare*, London: Faber & Faber, 1979.

32 S. J. Stone, 'The Church's one foundation is Jesus Christ her Lord', 1866.

33 Timothy Dudley-Smith, 'Lord, for the years' © 1969, Hope Publishing. Used by permission.